the g
of sodom

CREATION

The Ghosts Of Sodom
Marquis de Sade
ISBN 1 84068 101 2
Translated by John Phillips

Published 2003 by Creation Books
www.creationbooks.com

Contents

Translator's Preface

Sade's Charenton diaries were first published in France in 1970, following their discovery in the Sade family archives. They consist of two *cahiers* or notebooks, the first of which covers the period June 1807 to August 1808, the second 18th July to 30th November, 1814. The second notebook, then, extends to just two days before Sade's death on December 2nd, 1814. Other surviving material from the Charenton years include a small number of letters (Pauvert reprints fourteen of these which include the 'Final Proposals Made to My Family' of 1805 and the much commented 'Last Will and Testament' of 1806) and notes for *The Days At Florbelle*, Sade's only libertine work of the period the manuscript of which was ordered to be burnt by Sade's younger son, Donatien-Claude-Armand, together with some other documents which he considered might cause embarrassment to the family.

The letters Sade wrote from prison from 1778 up to his release in 1790 have been extensively worked on. The Charenton letters and diaries, however, have in the past attracted little critical attention and no systematic English translation of this material has been published before. Even Sade's notes on *The Days At Florbelle* have drawn little more than passing comment from even the most assiduous of Sade scholars. This new edition will, then, make available to readers of English writing that could in the past be accessed by readers of French alone. There may be a number of reasons for this neglect, and I will suggest three main ones. Firstly, the diary entries themselves are often notoriously hard to interpret, full of puzzling and enigmatic abbreviations, mysterious allusions, infuriating non-sequiturs and coded or veiled uses of language and, especially, of numbers. All of these features present both critic and translator with serious challenges. Secondly, only two of the four cahiers that originally made up Sade's diary output during the Charenton years have survived, numbers 2 and 3 having no doubt been destroyed. Georges Daumas draws our attention to the chronological discontinuity between these two documents: between the first cahier of 1807-8 and the fourth of 1814.[1] Daumas conjectures that no 2 was confiscated by the police (Pauvert adds that this probably occurred on June 5th 1807) and that no 3 was seized, together with other writings (eg, the manuscript of a play entitled *La Tour Mystérieuse*) by M. de Coulmier's successor as director of the hospice, Roulhac du Maupas when he assumed the post in June 1814. du Maupas did not share Coulmier's liberal and progressive approach to the treatment of patients and was far less sympathetic to Sade himself. The surviving cahiers leave the intervening years from August 1808 to July 1814 in relative darkness.[2] These lacunae make for an unsatisfying lack of continuity and a much reduced corpus, both factors that may have hitherto deterred critics and publishers alike. Thirdly and most importantly, the material content of both letters and diaries appears, at first sight at least, to offer little real meat to the critical palate. The diaries in particular seem dominated by tedious and repetitive accounts of Sade's life at Charenton, the pathetic details of his stormy relationship with its director, François Simonet de Coulmier, his constant lack of money to buy wood and other necessities, his preoccupation with putative release-dates, the comings and goings of family and other visitors, and of his devoted companion, Constance Quesnet. Such features are indicative of character-traits already well known to readers of Sade: a growing persecution-complex, an obsessive focus on the secret meanings of numbers, a compulsion to write (novels and plays in addition to the diaries and correspondence) and the considerable energies which he devoted to dramatic endeavours in the asylum. But this material also raises intriguing and important questions relating to the marquis's state of mind and creative abilities in his declining years, including the fundamental issue of the very status of the diaries themselves: that is, were they private accounts written only for the marquis himself and of little interest to the reader, or were they intended for posterity as an integral part of Sade's creative output?

There are sufficient similarities between the content of the *Florbelle Notes* and features of Sade's lost work, *The One Hundred And Twenty Days Of Sodom*, to infer that he was attempting to recreate it, at least in parts. The château of Florbelle recalls Silling as the site of orgies, in which victims are locked in cages, subjected to a number of atrocious torments and finally executed. Both titles link theme and geographical location to libertinism (the sub-title of Florbelle is: *ou les Égarements du libertinage (or the*

Deviations of Libertinism)), both works contain scenes of extreme violence, depictions of incestuous relations between the libertines and their sisters and daughters, scenes of black humour (children strapped to bombs and rockets), bestiality and many other perversions familiar to the reader of the *120 Days*, Sade's catalogue of sexual passions. One major difference, however: while the obscene and violent content of the *120 Days Of Sodom* is evident from a title that alludes directly both to the capital offence of sodomy and to the destruction of the Old Testament city by a wrathful deity, the title of *The Days At Florbelle* resists any such interpretation. Indeed, the proper name 'Florbelle' itself carries agreeable connotations (no doubt intentionally ironic) of floral beauty. Apart from the possibilities of a biting irony, Sade may well have selected this neutral title as a defensive strategy: such wording would have been less likely to arouse the suspicions of a warder or other person in authority, or even of his own sons, who might happen to glance casually at the title page of Sade's manuscript.

Jean-Jacques Pauvert, in his introduction to the French edition of the *Florbelle Notes*, makes clear his view that the writing of this whole period is inferior in quality to that of earlier times, that in the septuagenarian Sade especially, the literary flame is slowly dying. I want to examine the validity of this view in what follows.

With regard to the *Florbelle Notes*, it seems to me unfair to draw any firm conclusions regarding a writer's talent from a series of highly schematic notes covering little more than twenty pages in which the chief concern is the mechanics of plot, the number of characters, their names, their appearance in the narrative and other largely technical details. In any case, Pauvert himself argues quite persuasively that these notes (dated 1806-7) were actually part of a process of revision of a novel written years earlier, probably between 1799 and 1801, and so are surely unreliable as evidence of Sade's state of mind in the 1800s.

As for the diaries and letters, they could not be more different from each other in style and character. Whereas the diaries appear to make obfuscation into a virtue, the letters on the other hand are written with a clarity and elegance indicative of a lucid intelligence and an intense desire to communicate. This, one might say, is hardly surprising since, unlike the journals, they are obviously intended to be read by others and, for the most part, are concerned with financial and other matters of a practical importance to Sade. Of the fourteen letters reproduced in the Pauvert *Complete Works*, two are addressed to his lawyer, Gaufridy, one to Fouché, minister of police, and another to Napoléon requesting his release, two to M. de Coulmier, director of Charenton, concerning the amateur theatricals that Sade orchestrated at the asylum, a further three to Coulmier regarding matters touching upon Sade's accommodation and material conditions, one to Coulmier's successor, M. Roulhac du Maupas, requesting the restoration of access to the daily newspaper, one to the administration of the Théâtre-Français accompanying the submission of a 5-act tragedy, and one, the very last letter Sade would write, addressed to a M. Pépin, a tenant-farmer on Sade family property at Saumane, regarding the sale of wood to provide the ever indigent marquis with much needed funds — a pathetic note upon which to close Sade's extraordinarily unhappy life. The remaining two are testamentary in nature: the first addressed to Charles Quesnet, son of Sade's female companion, Constance, urges Charles to value his mother's affection and indeed her very existence (a positive view of motherhood which seems at odds with the hypothesis of mother-hatred in his fiction advanced by some critics[3]), and while there is no evidence of the context in which this brief letter was composed or the motivations behind it, the entire tone of the piece suggests a valedictory exhortation to the son to take care of his mother after Sade's death.[4] The second, entitled 'Final Proposals to My Family', is dated 24th August, 1805 by Pauvert and sets out detailed conditions for the signing of a contract, probably testamentary in nature, put to Sade by his family. Pauvert places it chronologically immediately before Sade's *Last Will And Testament* of the 30th January, 1806. None of these letters shows any signs of a dimming of Sade's intelligence, on the contrary, even those written in 1813 and 1814 reveal a sharpness of mind and a life-long gift for rhetoric, while the *Last Proposals*... and the *Will* that follows it demonstrate that, when it comes to money and property at least, Sade has lost none of his customary shrewdness or logic.

Sade is still, for instance, able to call upon his considerable play-acting talents when it serves his purposes, shifting tone from one letter to another accordingly. At times obsequious, as in his pleading letter to Napoléon ('He dares to consider himself, Sire, with the very deepest respect, Your Majesty's most humble and most obedient servant and subject.'), citing his son's distinguished military service and exaggerating his own advanced age and failing health ('He is a septuagenarian, nearly blind, afflicted with gout and rheumatism in his chest and stomach which cause him to suffer horrible pains'.... Sade was not quite 70 when he wrote this). At other times, an old aristocratic superciliousness rises to the surface and his tone can be haughty and imperious, as in this terse note to M. de Coulmier:

I have the honour to greet Monsieur de Coulmier, and I entreat him to leave me the man he has given me, and not to make me suffer the nuisance, which I find appalling, of seeing a different face every day.

SADE

It is interesting to note that, although Sade for the most part signs these letters without the aristocratic 'de' — a habit he felt obliged to assume during the years of the Revolution — there are two exceptions to this rule: the letter to Napoléon referred to earlier, and the final letter to the Saumane tenant. In both cases, Sade would obviously have wished to emphasise his noble origins. On the other hand, one cannot help feeling that there is a touch of wry self-irony in the 'change of face' remark. Sade is never so funny as when he appears to be taking himself seriously. This letter recalls many he wrote to his wife, Renée Pelagie, years earlier at the very start of his years of imprisonment in the late 1770s and 1780s. The following is one of many instances in which the marquis bitterly complains about his living conditions. The complaint is heart-felt but made with a dry sense of humour:

To Madame de Sade, 4th October, 1778

As for my cell, 'tis one more act to add to the others, and one I shall remember. Not only shall I be unable to have a fire throughout the winter, but, to boot, I am devoured by rats and mice, which keep me from getting a single minute of rest all night long. I have just spent six sleepless nights in a row, and when I ask if they would kindly have a cat put into the next room to destroy them, they answer that animals are forbidden. To which I respond: 'Why, fools that you are, if animals are forbidden, rats and mice should be forbidden, too.' To which they reply: 'That's different.'[5]

The diaries present their reader with more complex problems than the letters of either period. The obsession with numbers, the paranoid fear of being mistreated and despoiled by family, authorities, and even those close to him are familiar to readers of the letters from Vincennes and the Bastille in the 1780s, and it would be superfluous to rehearse these features in any detail. However, it is worth making two observations with regard to them and to the question of Sade's mental stability at this time. Firstly, what Sade counts more than anything else is the visits he receives from family and friends, — an understandable preoccupation on the part of a prisoner, perhaps, — Armand's, his cousin's, and especially, those of his young lover, Magdeleine Leclerc, and even the significance he attaches to these numbers of coded messages being passed to him pertaining to his release may not exactly qualify as a symptom of insanity when one considers the censorship and searches to which Sade was indeed subjected and which he may have thought those close to him were attempting to circumvent. Secondly, as mentioned above, searches of his rooms resulted in the confiscation and destruction of an unknown quantity of material, including the *Florbelle* manuscript and the two missing diary notebooks, and his freedom to walk in the asylum gardens had been curtailed for a period of time. Following Coulmier's replacement by the far less amenable du Maupas, the marquis was eventually deprived of all writing materials. It is also a matter of record that both of his sons attempted to manipulate their father in August 1808 in the matter of marriage contracts. If Sade was obsessional, as many prisoners are, then this paranoia had its roots in reality.

In addition to the issue of Sade's sanity, the in some ways related issue of the status of the diaries themselves is paramount. It has hitherto been assumed that, given the coded nature of the writing, Sade could only have been writing for himself, that, in other words, this was an intimate, personal record of daily events to which he alone would have access: 'It is clear that M. de Sade was writing for himself alone, and with precaution, and that he alone could understand himself.'[6] The style of the diary writing would appear to support this view. As Georges Daumas points out, entries seem to have been composed in haste, they are replete with misspellings and there is little punctuation: 'Everywhere we can see the tired, clumsy or uncertain hand of an old man'.[7] At times, the words cascade breathlessly into long Proustian or better, Wolfian sentences in which thoughts and emotions whirl together confusingly. This impression of confusion of thought and language is due also to the almost complete lack of punctuation in some entries.

The water is muddied further by a profusion of abbreviations of proper names, by the use of pseudonyms, some identifiable, others difficult to decipher, and by frequent and obscure allusions. The following two extracts illustrate well all of these features:

On the 17th Moses and Md. go to see the D. de V...
On the 18th in the morning I receive a letter from the doctor promising to send his virgin again on the 21st.

On the 27th, Md. goes to Paris to see B.S. and Pal: She is displeased with the former and pleased with the latter. In agreement with the people she has seen, she prescribes a course of conduct for me which I am going to observe. As regards Boursier, he agrees to advance the 1st month only. Paquet comes on that day and says that the work has been found good, but that circumstances etc...... he has lodged it with Testu and will come and deliver a response to me without fail on Thursday 4th or Thursday 11th.

It is too easy to dismiss such passages as the infantile ramblings of a senile old man. The obscure and carelessly written nature of passages like these would admittedly appear to support the view of Daumas and others that Sade was writing only for himself. And yet, much of this was perhaps intended as a screen against police censorship. Moreover, in the case of a author whose every word is chosen to project a particular self-construct, and indeed to defend him in the sight of others, the hypothesis of a journal not intended sooner or later for public consumption is hard to credit. There are many instances in which the personal diaries of authors and other artists are clearly composed to be read as part of a wider corpus of work. In Sade's case, the dialogic and indeed frequently conative nature of his expression suggests at the very least a recognition that all writing is in essence a communicative act. Either Sade was by this stage truly a split-personality, condition exhibited in the very construction of his discourse, or the old habit of addressing a reader informs, either consciously or unconsciously, the character and expression of his thoughts:

Of Magdeleine Leclerc: 'Examine carefully her coldness, her insouciance in pleasure and in conversations, and in these you will see irrefutable proof of what I am suggesting'

It is well known that Sade was in the habit of addressing himself in his personal writings as 'vous', a characteristic particularly noticeable in the *Notes On The Days At Florbelle*, where Sade is effectively composing aide-mémoires to remind him to make certain changes to his manuscript. In diary entries like this one, however, where there is a clear split between the writing 'I' and the reading 'you', a process of far greater subtlety is at work. Not an aide-mémoire and still less a plausible symptom of schizophrenia, the dialogic nature of entries such as this builds a reader into the text itself. Like the letters Sade wrote from Vincennes and the Bastille and indeed the letters which were contemporaneous with them, Sade's diaries were intended to be read, and not only by the censorious authorities who might monitor and confiscate them.

Sade's intense desire to leave behind a legacy of writing that would explain his situation and vindicate him in the eyes of future readers is a primary motivation behind the diaries as well as behind many of the letters he wrote during this period. The whole notion of legacy in relation to Sade has been treated in some depth by Geoffrey Bennington in his article, 'Forget to Remember, Remember to Forget: Kant avec Sade'. Bennington reminds us that, for Jacques Derrida, all writing is in essence testamentary, and so we might say that 'reading is in essence about sorting out and understanding legacies'.[8] Bennington argues that in his formal will, Sade generates a double bind within the structure of inheritance or legacy itself, whereby he instructs his inheritors to prepare his tomb in such a way that it leaves no trace, to make sure that his memory disappears, or in other words, to remember to forget to remember. For Bennington, this is a classical double bind situation:

Let's try to hear the full ambivalence of these formulations: forget to remember says not just: don't remember, forget it in the sense of omitting to do it (which is already a double bind in that the injunction requires its addressee to remember to forget to remember, to remember not to remember), but also: forget in order to remember, as a better way of remembering. And symmetrically, 'remember to forget' says not only: don't omit to forget, keep in mind that you must forget (which is again a double bind in that you must forget but must not forget (to forget)), but also remember in order to forget.[9]

Like the will, the diaries are set to self-destruct, or put another way, they appear programmed to conceal rather than reveal. As I have already implied, the basis of my argument here is that, contrary to all appearances, any diary writer intends sooner or later to be read. But Sade plays a game of hide and seek with a reader who is not supposed to exist, just as the inheritors of his will must remember not to remember. Despite their obfuscations and concealments, their obscure allusions and enigmatic expressions, the diaries constantly reach out to their reader for sympathy and understanding. In fact, other than himself, Sade at different times apostrophizes specific readers: his dead father, for example, or Constance Quesnet during her illness. That these particular implied readers would never become real readers does not detract from the reader-centredness of the writing. In their self-justificatory function, then, as in their essential literariness and teasing enigmas, the diaries are no different from many of his fictional writings. In this sense, they are no more and no less testamentary than any other part of the Sadean corpus.... which brings us back to the observation by Derrida that writing is itself a form of testament. What is meant here is not the disposition of land and property, but the much more fundamental question of Sade's spirit, as disseminated throughout his oeuvre. But what exactly has Sade left us in the Charenton diaries?: nothing less than his remains in their literal sense, that is, what is left of Sade the man, which amounts to saying that Sade's legacy is the very act of bequeathing. I use the word 'act' also in its theatrical sense, because Sade's most important bequest is his awareness of role-playing and the recognition underlying that awareness that behind all of the masks that one is obliged to wear (social, psychological, emotional), an authentic, unconstucted self may not exist at all.

This role-playing facility makes it hard not to see many aspects of the diaries as in some way staged or self-consciously performed for the benefit of those real readers who might eventually read them.

Among the many roles or masks the author of these diaries may be said to assume are those of the devoted partner on the one hand and the promiscuous and ageing Casanova on the other. In Cahier 1 (1808), there is an appearance of genuine concern when Constance Quesnet falls ill. At this point, Sade becomes the caring nursemaid and anxious lover. Cahier 4, written six years later, nevertheless speaks of a sexual relationship with a young woman of 17, the 17 year old laundry-maid, Magdeleine Leclerc, that apparently began years earlier and so may well have been in existence at the time of Constance's illness. It is difficult to reconcile these conflicting selves, both of which, taken singly, display aspects of Sade's character that are highly sympathetic: the affair with Magdeleine which was certainly, at its outset at least, little more than a financial arrangement seems to have had an emotional dimension as well, and there is always an element of pathos in the picture of an old man possessively pursuing a young girl, quizzing her about her movements, reacting jealously at the thought of a younger rival.[10] So which is the real Sade? Constance's devoted companion or her faithless lover? a Lothario whose sexual energies were seemingly unabated in the last decade of his life, a love-sick buffoon or a ruthless abuser of innocence deserving only of our contempt? While the author seeks to project self-images that are positive and sympathetic (his legacy), we his readers and inheritors may inherit quite different images, that he never intended to bequeath.

Nevertheless, the enigmas of the text challenge the reader to find an authentic self. It is no coincidence that two of the codes most often used in Sade's text are directly related to the two dominant preoccupations of his entire system of thought: religion and sex.

On a number of occasions in the first cahier, he refers to himself as 'Moïse' or Moses. Given Sade's constant attacks in his novels and essays on religion in general and Christianity in particular, there is obvious irony in this self-stylisation as the father of Judeo-Christianity. Interestingly, Bennington views the very business of reading and interpretation, of hermeneutics, as a *filial* situation:

For this hermeneutic way of dealing with the situation of reading which I am suggesting just is a situation of legacy, the situation is a filial one: the text is the word of the father (whoever wrote the text is in the position of father with respect to whomsoever places him or herself in the hermeneutic position with respect to it), or, if you prefer, the word of God.[11]

In this perspective, we, Sade's readers and inheritors, are unavoidably positoned as his sons and daughters. The name Moses also carries associations with a form of writing (The Ten Commandments) that is itself God's legacy to Man. If Sade is a new Moses, then, it is because he is leaving mankind a legacy not from God but from man, a law not of the spirit but of the flesh.

Which leads us to consider a code Sade employs in both cahiers, but especially in cahier 4 in the context of his relationship with Magdeleine Leclerc. The following entry illustrates the enigmatic use of an ancient symbol: 'On the 15th Prosper comes with the idea of Ø Ø. It is his 3rd visit and his maid's second, forming Ø for the first time.' Francine Du Plessix-Gray considers that the symbol is a reference to sodomy.[12] Whether or not its meaning is as precise as this, the symbol is taken from medieval heraldry where it is associated with the taboo and so it clearly refers here to sexual activity of some sort.

While the adoption of the pseudonym, Moses, exhibits Sade's gift for self-dramatisation, the heraldic symbol is ludic and inventive. But these and other examples of coded expression also suggest a desire to fictionalise his experience designed to protect him from the censor. A pragmatic response to the constraints of Sade's situation and the ludicity and inventiveness of art are, after all, not incompatible.

This inventiveness, which is itself evidence of a desire to please the reader, can be found in many other features of style in the diaries. There is, for example, a talent for wry and self-ironising observation, as in this scathing witticism directed at his family (referred to obliquely as M.F.): 'The thermometer of M. F. is set for rain.' There is, too, an acute sense of the absurdity of his situation and perhaps of life in general. The following entry which is ostensibly dictated by Sade's counting mania might have been written by Ionesco: 'On the 18th at 9 o'clock, the clock strikes 26 times.'

Conclusion: Life Imitates Art

Sade's diary entries concerning his liaison with the 17 year-old Magdeleine Leclerc during the final months of his life are interesting, as I have said, for what they may reveal about Sade's emotional state of mind. But the real interest here lies in the construction of these accounts. This has not escaped the attention of Neil Shaeffer who, in his recent biography of Sade, observes:

The reader may note that Sade divided his sessions with Magdeleine Leclerc into conversation, sex acts ("the pleasures"), and instruction. This is the formula of all of his erotic novels, in which a girl (Magdeleine was young enough to be his granddaughter), willing or not, is indoctrinated into the libertine mind and body. In this final romance with Magdeleine Leclerc, Sade relived in a sometimes tender, sometimes poignant form the essential dream of his long and tortured life.[13]

Sade may well have been acting out fantasies so often elaborated in his fictions, as Shaeffer here suggests, but the current of influence can also be reversed, that is, Sade cannot help but narrativise these events which for him in part means ordering and classifying them. There is also a writerly sense of detail and at times a characteristically Sadean use of cliché. The following is Sade's final entry relating to the girl, penned only days before his death. Note, even in this brief account, the desire to tell a story which is less about Magdeleine than about Sade himself, his pain both physical and emotional, about his fears and insecurities, and also about his sexual satisfaction expressed in a punch-line that brings down the curtain on a scene replete with sensibilities:

On the 27th, Mgl. came on her 96th (visit). She seemed to be most sympathetic to my pains which I described to her in detail. She had not been to a single ball and promised not to go to any, spoke of the future, said that she would be 18 years old on the 19th of next month, lent herself as usual to our little games, promised to come back next Sunday or Monday, thanked me for what I was doing for her, and made it clear that she was not unfaithful to me, nor had she any desire to be. During this visit, Varennes brought back a reply from M. Roze who was going to put the men to work. Mgl. stayed for 2 hours, and I was very pleased with the session.

During her visit, Mg.: all the libertinism of the balls of Rousseau.

So Sade appears to end his life in a manner resembling all too closely that of his fictitious anti-hero in 'Dialogue BetweenA Priest And A Dying Man' who indulges in the pleasures of the body while the body is still able to feel pleasure. And yet, is this perhaps simply another self-dramatising moment? The 'balls of Rousseau' metaphor comes as an afterthought, we note, as a line of closure, less of his life than of the narration of it. Like the many abbreviations and coded references, its enigmatic character resists interpretation. The very idea of a Rousseau ball is a contradiction in terms — the Calvinist philosopher was notoriously puritanical — an oxymoron thrown at Sade's implied reader in a final gesture of joyful defiance. We shall never know exactly what libertine practices Sade enjoyed with Magdeleine Leclerc because the narrator chooses, here as on so many other occasions in the diaries as well as in his novels and other fictions, not to say everything. It is, I contend, Sade's awareness of the reader that prevents him from doing so. If there is to be room for the workings of the reader's imagination, the author-narrator of *The New Justine* insists in footnote, then something must always be left out:

'Things are better expressed by being suppressed,' La Mettrie writes somewhere, 'desire is stimulated by arousing curiosity about a partly hidden object, which cannot yet be perceived, but which one wants to be able to perceive.'
This is why we throw a veil over scenes the content of which we do no more than suggest'.[14]

Note On Translation

In the diaries, Sade is cavalier with punctuation which is often notable by its absence. Where I have judged it helpful for the reader, I have repunctuated the text in accordance with the writer's apparent intentions. On the other hand, there is a blatent lack of consistency in the diaries in the use of verb-tenses, so that Sade alternates continually between past and present, even on occasions within the same sentence. I have respected this idiosyncrasy in most cases.

NOTES

1 See Jean-Jacques Pauvert's introduction to the diaries in the French edition edited by Pauvert and Le Brun: *Oeuvres Complètes du Marquis de Sade*, Tome Onzième, Société Nouvelle des Éditions Pauvert, 1991, pp. 95-97.

2 A half dozen or so letters written by Sade during this period do provide some insight into his main preoccupations: theatre performances, the staging of his own plays in Paris, limitations placed on his freedom of movement at the asylum, and the ever-present longing to be free: see later.

3 See, for example, Jane Gallop, 'Sade, Mothers, and Other Women' in *Sade And The Narrative Of Transgression*, edited by Allison, Roberts and Weiss, (Cambridge University Press, 1995), pp. 122-141.

4 Pauvert points out that this is a draft and may never have actually been sent. It is not dated.

5 Richard Seaver, *Marquis de Sade: Letters From Prison* (The Harvill Press, 2000), p. 83.

6 Pauvert, *Notice Bibliographique*, pp. 95-6, quoting George Daumas, op.cit.

7 Quoted by Pauvert, op. cit.

8 Geoffrey Bennington, 'Forget To Remember, Remember To Forget: *Sade Avec Kant*' in Phillips, J. (ed.), 'Sade And His Legacy', special number of *Paragraph*, Vol. 23, No. 1 (March 2000), pp. 75-86; this reference p. 75.

9 Ibid., p. 77.

10 The unfortunately named Lefevre. Some twenty-five years earlier in 1781, Sade had become insanely jealous of his wife, Renée-Pelagie, whom he accused of conducting a sexual affair with a servant of hers named Lefevre. Now, Sade suspected the young Magdeleine of also betraying him with a man of the same name.

11 Op. cit., p. 75.

12 Francine Du Plessix-Gray, *At Home With The Marquis de Sade* (Penguin Books, 1998), p. 406.

13 Neil Shaeffer, *The Marquis de Sade* (Picador, 2001), p. 512; first published by Alfred A. Knopf, 1999.

14 *La Nouvelle Justine* (Union Générale d'Éditions, 1978), vol.2, p. 251, note 6; my translation.

The Charenton Diaries

THE FIRST NOTEBOOK: 5 JUNE 1807 to 26 AUGUST 1808

DIARY

(This Diary is a sequel to those that have been taken from me)

The Year 1807

At nearly two o'clock on the 5th, Mr de Coul enters my room, followed by three policemen, one of whom was Vera, the Inspector General who read me an order by the Prefect containing an injunction to seize all my papers, which was done without prior inspection. When I objected that they were taking away documents that were extremely important to me such as receipts, bills, etc., I was told that they did not have time to inspect them but that they would send back those ones that were important to me! While they were carrying out this operation in my quarters, they were doing the same in Md.'s, taking from her also her most important papers. They took from her those manuscripts that I had produced in and rescued from the Bastille and carried them all off. At first, the Chief of Police behaved quite harshly towards me, but later his manner softened and he assured me that there would be no repercussions. They placed everything in a coach and went off with it all.[1]

This operation took place exactly six years and three months after I was first detained and 4 years and six weeks, or 4 years and 39 days, since I came to Charenton[2]. My poor daughter[3] was most affected by this blow, and this caused me all the more pain in that I have no friend dearer to me in all the world.

After this business, Mr de C. came to see us for an hour to console us, and I was most pleased with him. On this very same day, I had just installed my new writing-desk. This event took place 3 years 1 month and 5 days after the previous one.[4]

On the evening of the 6th, I went to see Mr de C. who in no way reassured me as to the consequences of this event and who assured me that it was they who had spread frightful ideas about everything that they took away. On the 7th and 8th, I saw Mr de C. and was perfectly happy with him.

On the 9th, I wrote him a carefully reasoned letter, in accordance with what we had decided together. Md. was to go to Paris, and that's where she was.

On the 10th, I lodged the letter as evidence of the confiscated papers with Mr de Coulm. He leaves for Paris on the 11th.

On the 12th, C. returned and calmed my fears. On the same day, Desfossés came on what I believe was his 3rd visit. We told him nothing.

On Sunday 14th, Allard gave me his bill for the writing-desk amounting to 99 [frs].[5]

On the 14th, François came for the second time and still did not bring me what he had promised.

On Monday 15th, Md. goes to Paris. I am

informed on the evening of the 16th that she may not return until the 18th.

On the 17th, Md. comes back from Peking and gives Moses a little sugar concerning his fables. Attention is drawn to the 4th, the 3rd (see what this is). On the same evening, F... talks to Moses and does not give him as much sugar. He uses spiced vinegar in a quite uncalled-for way, but in the end says that the milk will not be changed, that he has seen Groseille who has promised to go ahead. He asserted to Moses that the last 3 fables were done in Meudon, which is not true, that he intended to sell the fables, which is as false as it is absurd, and in consequence, [that] Moses was a *rascal* a *rogue* a *wretch*, all spices both charming and well conceived. F... also told Moses that he had been told to be more difficult about the lemons sold to Moses. He also said that Md. de l'Orme had been suspected of being involved in these dealings, a truly awful and revolting calumny. After all, there is a huge difference between Md. de Lorme's version and that of M.F.[6]

On the same day, a snout had come to dine at the house and had said that he had been told that Darling took a great interest in Moses.[7]

On the 19th, I went to sign the Arles letter and was most pleased with F... I submitted a second fable in evidence.

On the 25th, 1500 [frs] are received from Aubert.

On the 26th, he meets Varennes[8] going to fetch my breakfast and forbids him to do so on the pretext that he objects to it. I hurry to speak to him and make it up with him. Now this was just a f....[9] because he knew very well that Varennes had been in my service for a long time. He asks why I don't eat in my bedchamber.

On the 30th, he changed the time of rehearsals and this change ruined everything I had stipulated.

July

On the 1st and 2nd, there was a lot of talk of going against my wishes and replacing Varenne with Pémat, and I noticed that the expressions of the boss and those around him had changed and become cold. L. told me many things that convinced me how much everything that had happened had been my undoing.

On the 3rd, Mr Oliver's agent came to bring me 300 [fr.]. He was prevented from speaking to me and sent away, Md. had to run after him. When I complained to him about this treatment, he told me that complaints had been made about him to the police regarding my correspondence, which made me realise that they believed this woman to be something else.

He also told me that a frightful letter attacking Md. and myself as well as several other people in the house had been written to the Archbishop, that it was an anonymous letter written in copperplate which leads me to suspect a priest who's been here by the name of Poincot.

On the 4th, everything seemed to go better and the c.r.é[10] put my mind at rest.

Md. leaves for Paris on the 6th and is due to return on the 9th. The cabinet-maker comes to bring me my writing-desk on the 7th. He is told that in order to see me he must obtain permission from Dumoustier and he comes to my rooms only after speaking to the said Dumoustier.[11]

Md. came back on the evening of the 9th with quite good fables. On the same day, C. received quite bad ones in action with Moses.

On the 11th, Desfosses and Robert came to dinner unexpectedly. The kitchen was forbidden to do anything unusual. Both went off after dinner in a manner that was as rude as it was extraordinary.

On the 11th, I learn of the death of Md.

Bouchard.

On the 18th at 9 o'clock, the clock strikes 26 times.

On the 19th, three persons, a mother and her two daughters, came to dine with us. They took us by surprise and there again was the number 19 and the number 3.

On the 20th, the number 24 is conspicuous.

On the 21st, they again threaten to take Varenne away from me.

On the 29th, I read the play which I have written for Mr. de Coulmier's name-day to the whole assembly (including Md. Santeuil). In the evening, idea Ø[12] at 116, the 4th of the year.

On the 31st, Md. goes to Paris.

August

On the 2nd, lots of 2s come to the fore: I was sent two newspapers, two citizens of Mazan[13] came to see me, etc....

On the 3rd, Md. Populus came to tell Madame to come and fetch her papers. I was informed that I would have mine in a little while but not before *the holidays*.

Md. leaves for Paris to get her papers on the 3rd.

On the 7th, Md. comes back. She has been given back her fables and they said to her that Moses would not get his immediately, because of their length.

On the 9th, Cat. comes with the girl he is to marry to bring me the 7th payment.

On the same day, Md. P. and her daughter came to dinner. The number 2 was strongly emphasised.

On the 11th, the 2 men from Provence came to dine with us and brought 3 bottles of their wine.

On the 18th, the 3 men from Provence come to see me for the 3rd time. One of them was leaving for Provence, taking my accounts with him, assuring me that he would do all he could to get payment for me.

On the 21st, I had been suffering from terrible insomnia for 3 we[eks], and it was on the night of the 20th to the 21st that I thought what bad luck my plays had always brought me.

The Hesdin plays were interrupted by the death of a grandmother whom I adored and who had brought me up.

Those planned for the Ma[rech]al de Segur and his family were interrupted by the Arcueil affair.

The Mazan plays by the Aix affair.

The two plays that I am putting on now are experiencing problems.

The one that I am staging in Versailles is also having different kinds of problems.

While the Charenton play is being performed, they search my rooms turning them upside down, etc...

On the evening of the 25th, Md. had a violent attack of cramps. Th: and I watched over her all night.

On the 29th, Savine brings two men to me, one of whom offers to be of service to me in all my affairs and asks me to give power of attorney to Savine. I did no such thing.

Month of September

On the 20th and 23rd Prosper writes again.

On the 23rd, it's for the Langot woman who wants to get her husband a position here.

On the 17th Savine came. He said he'd found what was needed for the 2 objects.

On the 23rd, I receive a letter from Aubert promising 3000 [fr.] in two postings. (Therefore the letter which I did not date must have been received in the first 8 days of October since he dated his the 11th).
October

On the 2nd, Mr. de C. came to Md. Q's to say that he did not want the play that had been in rehearsal for a month and that I had written for him to be performed. This inflamed tempers a little on both sides. (I wanted to tear up the work). Leon was brought out to direct The Huntsmen which was performed instead, and my couplets which I was asked to place in a new context had to be sung.

On the same evening, my elder son wrote to tell me that he was coming to see me on the 3rd.

It was *on the 3rd that the piece was performed*, therefore the farce is from the 2nd to the 3rd.

He did indeed come. It was M. de Coulmier's name-day, but he did not stay for the whole performance (he did likewise the following year).

On the 5th, the Langot woman comes but warned by me in advance, Mr. de C. refuses her at my entreaty. She had come to find a situation for her husband here.

M. C. was extremely honest with me about this.

On the 12th, he gives me 200 [fr.] of the money he has belonging to me and signs a bill for me on the 16th for a quarter of the wood I need for the winter.

On the evening of the 12th, he came to see us at Md. Quenet's. Moses had asked to go for a walk, and he did not wish it. (It was the day when he put on the Louvigni farce).

On the 16th, the elder son paid me another surprise visit. They did not seem inclined, he said, to accede to my request. He said that he was perhaps going away for two months to Germany. He had dinner with me.

Md. Quesnet had been in Paris since the 14th.

On the 17th, Md. comes back ill from Paris, feeling the effects of her deafness. She brings Mr Vau's wife with her, who leaves the following day. She has not achieved any of the things I wanted.

On the night of the 24th to the 25th, I dreamt that my rooms were being searched and that all my books were being turned upside down.

On the 27th, I receive a letter from my youngest after six months of silence.

On Saturday the 31st, the Robin woman turns up. I ask her for fresh supplies, she says that she will discuss it with her husband and that she will write to me.

November

On the evening of the 3rd, Md. asks for 6 f[r] for the lottery.

On the 5th, the new haberdasher arrives. He comes from Troyes.

On the 8th, Lenormand[14] sends his 10th payment and a 200 [fr] note payable on February the 15th for Varennes.

On the morning of the 11th, Alex: talks of lib. according, he says, to the Po:.[15]

The 12th: the eldest writes on the 10th that he will come to dinner on the 12th, the same day. He did indeed come, the number 1 came up all day long, and it was my eldest's third since his return. The 1st[16] of The Crimes of Love was returned to me. He lent me the 1 of The History of France, he had written on the 10th. We were served 1 extra dish at dinner, etc..... However, I was told in the evening that C... had said and done several things against Moses. Md. took her 1st music lesson, the Po: remained outside 1 more day. My son spoke of his 1st volume. He said that there is talk of me in newspaper articles and that in view of this, they were thinking of moving me further away. He said that Md. de Talaru[17] is ill and that he is leaving for Echaufour. He makes it quite clear this time that it is the family doing everything.

On the 14th, Vergne and one of his friends come to see me, Vergne says that the Sabin affair is going well and that Asselin wishes to renew his opposition. They draw attention to no. 2.

The same evening, Courtois sends 300 [fr.] I see two men in the morning, I receive 300 [fr.] (in the evening). Vergne drew attention to no. 7 and it is the 1st time I see this man.

On Friday the 20th, the youngest came, asking for an authority over Lenormand to pay Asselin. I gave him 200 f[r] to take from Lenormand over the course of the year. As we were walking, he asked me where *my* cemetery was.

On the 30th, C. did and said some harsh and unpleasant things about the wood.

December

Instead of coming back on the 2nd on her usual day, Md. P. does not return until the 4th and says that the fables will only be given back if the family requests it. She leaves again on the 5th. She says that Moses's fa: will again be r., Moses who is here only through grace and out of consideration for M.F., for otherwise he would be at the G. M. She appears in a word very agitated and very out of breath. During all this time, M. F.'s thermometer shows rain.[18]

P. comes back on the 10th to say that she cannot stay.

On the same day of the 10th, I learn that it was Massé who produced the book of *My Seven-Year Persecution.*

On the 13th, a large gathering at the concert, including Doctor Gal. Md. sings 3 couplets by me on this occasion.

On the 16th, Md. goes to Paris and returns on the 19th.

On the 17th, the priest comes to see me.

On the 21st, Pop. writes to say that she cannot come back with us.

On the 26th, Lenormand sends 144 f[r] instead of 150 and the three louis from Madame.

On the 29th, they changed the woman who was above my head, they put another one in and the old one was put next door.

Reflexion

If the 16 months I did before the judgement are not counted in my detention, then I have done in my first period of detention only...........11 years 10 months
To complete the 20 years, are therefore remaining........
8 years 2 [months]
20 y[ears]

I therefore had 8 years 2 months to do when I entered Pelagie, as shown by the 28 of the Prefecture. So Charenton is 6 years 2 months or two months into the 7th year as shown by the 27th day of my arrival here and by the 3rd January 1808; another 17 months to do until the 3rd June 1809.
For the total of this second period of detention was........
8 years 2 months
with those already done.................... 11 years 10 months
to complete the 20 years.................................... 20 y[ears]
and having started on the 2nd April 1801 not including police-detention, this must necessarily take me to the 2nd June 1809. (Which today on the 2nd January 1808 gives me another 17 months exactly to do. This calculation is quite rigorous since it does not include even the police-detention or the Terror.)

On the 29th, I asked him if I could take the room above mine since it was vacant, he told me that I was too late and that this room was promised to a lady who did indeed arrive the same evening. (Becoming vacant five months later, I asked for it again, my request was again refused me[19]).

The year 1808

January

I dreamt during the night of the 31st to the 1st January that I found all my papers in the yard together with a large sum in ecus, I saw the ecus and the papers.

After 8 o'clock, I went up to embrace M. de C. who said some very agreeable things to me and gave me permission to go and see M. de Guise three times. (Which I made last until May).

That same day, the 1st January, M. de C. came to see Md. Quenet while I was there. Instead of bringing me the 24 oranges that I had asked for, I was brought between18 and 10 only. I got Md. to offer some to M. de C. who on the 1st of the month only took three, leaving 9 which makes for the most beautiful 13 and 9 possible.

Note regarding my wood

On January 3rd, I had burnt half of my ration and I had begun on the 24th October. This half therefore lasted 72 days, and if the other half goes as quickly I shall be short of wood by March 15th. Which means that I shall be without wood for 46 days. Now, to cover these 46 days, a further two carriage-loads are needed or 4 quarters which means that I shall have received 20 in all this winter.

Diary Continued

On the 7th, M. de C. sent for me to postpone the performance until the *17*th but it was just a piece of nonsense intended to give me a 17 and a 23. An absurdity repeated much too often, especially since the performance did not take place until much later. The calendar proves that it was a 7 and a 9.

On the 12th the doctor comes with his maid, it is his 2nd visit, there are two of them, he talks of *7 or 8*; there's *the 2* again with *the 7* but no idea that day.

On the 15th Prosper comes with the idea of Ø Ø. It is his 3rd visit and his maid's second, forming Ø for the first time.

On the 20th, Lenormand comes; he's been leasing now from me for 7 years and he has 23 years enjoyment left; see the result of the meeting in my papers.

On the 27th, Lenormand writes that he has received an attachment of 500 [fr.] sent by Després at the instigation of mistress Baudrais and that he *can no longer pay*.

On the 28th which is the anniversary of my father's death, I think of him all day long and go to bed shedding tears for him. Oh! if he were still alive, would he have tolerated all the absurdities of which I am a victim!!!

On the 29th, I wanted to recall the whole period of my detention; so, I was arrested in February 1777 and taken to No 11 at Vincennes.

I remain there......................................	1 year 4 months
I go to Aix in June 1778, Aix and my flight make up	3 months
I return to No 6 at Vincennes on the 7th September 1778 and I probably stay until September 1784..................	6 [years]
I am transferred from Vincennes to the Bastille in September 1784 and I remain in the Bastille[20] until the	

3rd July 1789...........................	4 [years] 10 [months]
I was transferred from the Bastille to Charenton on the 3rd July, 1789 and I remained there until the 3rd August, 1790[21]...	9 [months]
Total...	13 [years] 2 [months]

On the 29th, C. sent for me to attend a drama committee, he said, the result of which was that after what we were going to do, we would perform Claudine and the Tinker, and then in April, the Folies, etc.......and a play that would be chosen according to the talent of the new actors that would be given to me to train, but that Ambroise would not be staged, even though he had given his word of honour, which pained me greatly because of the sorrow this would cause Md. who wept about it all evening, and all this shows that I shall never be free of vexations; one way or another I am forever to be their victim.

On the 30th, notification of assignment from Md. Baudrai to M. Martin arrived, and I sent it immediately to M. Vergne.

On the evening of the 30th, M.C.'s abruptness.

On the 31st, Lenormand sends his 1st payment per plot of land.

February

On the 6th, my eldest comes still worrying about business matters and silent about Md.'s, does not contradict the idea of 7 years, is surprised that I am not performing the Comedy.

(He came two days into the 13th week since his last on the 12th November, the 85th day therefore after his 3rd; he did not come for 85, 3 months minus 5 days.)

On the evening of the 7th, I am given a letter from Courtois containing 300 [fr.] and an authority to sign for the cutting of the wood at Saumane.

On the 8th, M.C. told me that he does not despair to obtain my freedom but that I had to wait a while longer. Md. had left for Paris in the morning. He did not want me to rehearse a scene at the theatre on the day of the dress rehearsal. He spoke to me of a certain *Eudes* at the police who often came here and who knew me.

On the 11th, Md. comes back from Paris, my son says she had already been to the police before him and as he had spoken it had become futile for him to return there with her. She therefore went there on her own, did not hand in her authority and the only response she received was that the prefect would be notified but that I could only have the business papers here.

She had not seen Vergne, all of which proves that arrangements have been made and that they are waiting for the right time.

On the morning of the 13th, he sent for me to tell me that there would be no performance on Monday because of the bad weather, that what was supposed to be the dress rehearsal on Sunday would serve as performance and that I should write to cancel the tickets; all of which produced a situation identical to that of his name-day. He said that we would perform on the 3rd March.

On the 14th, M. de C. told me that we will restage the same performance on the 3rd March, which means 17 days after the other one and consequently establishes a superb *17 and 23*.

On the evening of the 15th, even though the previous night's performance had been perfect and I had taken a great deal of care over it, he made some fairly unpleasant remarks to me. He instructed me to tell Descamps that he did not want him to play in the Comedy any more. I told him this. The next day, the 16th, the said Descamps left in a mood and did not come back that night. He had been here 103 days, he had arrived on the 5th November and he does this on the 16th. All of these figures liken him prodigiously to Mand.

On the 26th, Robin's old clerk comes to see me and speaks to me of Robin's affairs.

The musician continued

He has been here 10 days exactly and 3 months, having arrived in November, 103 days ago; but he comes back *on the 17th* after 2 days when he stays for *3 weeks.*

On the 18th, I went to show M. de C. a letter from Arles containing the promise of money in May. He is very civil about it.

On the morning of the 20th, I receive a letter regarding the Beaudrai affair from a man named Trecour who claims to be Vergne's successor, and I answer it straightaway.

On the same day, Chaprot comes to tell me that Coul. has absolutely forbidden Md. Quesnet to sing at the concert, and he has done this both rudely and in a discourteous manner.

On the 22nd, I saw him on the matter, he accepted responsibility himself for this snub and told me to send Md. to him. She went to see him that evening and he did not speak to her about it. That same day, Diart came to see me and asked me how old Md. de Sade was.

On the 25th, Diart writes to tell me that a certain M. Trecour is indeed M. Vergne's successor and that this gentleman intends to come to see me on Sunday the 28th. I write to inform this gentleman that Md. Quenet will call to see him on Monday the 29th.

On the 25th, they brought the 3 act drama back to me, saying that Picard's had not wanted it, and I said to take it to the Francois.

March 1808

On the 1st, I write to Versailles for my monthly income. Lenormand writes back in a temper refusing to pay the bills, sending them back, including the one for a thousand francs which angers me. He says that he cannot pay any more because of the liens.

Md. goes to Paris on the 3rd to see M. Trecour with whom a letter had been lodged and who was expecting Md. on the 4th. *The 3 M: comes for the fables.*

On the 4th, idea Ø Ø appears the v. of 9 months.

On the 5th, I wait for Md. to return, she came back and said that M. Trecour would be coming as I wished on the 13th.

On the 9th, M. de C. had me come down on the pretext that as he was going to Paris, he wanted to know whether I had anything to tell him relating to the Comedy. There was a tall young man there who kept observing me. C. spoke to me quite civily, asked me if I had any errands for him in Paris, and he told me that the Comedy would be on the 17th. All in all, the whole thing was very much like Daigrefeuille's grand visit, the Bishop was also mentioned, etc.... he told me that the air at Charenton was excellent for me whereupon I replied that the air outside would suit me just as well, and he told me that he would do all he could to make my lot comfortable, and this stranger was watching me all the time.

On the 11th, Mr. Brise came to talk to Md. about her mortgages. He said that at de Loches's there were two bonds that were thought to be patent because the records were not at the notary's.

On the 13th, on my requisition, I saw M.

Trecour, Vergne's successor for the 1st time. He promised me he would do all he could to settle the Martin affair as well as the sale.

On the 15th, lect' esiepma. [*Reading of my play?*]

On the morning of the 20th, I hear about Lambert's death.

On the 21st, Md. tells me that she thinks my detention will not end until I am 70 years old, the age at which a prisoner can no longer be held. The cobbler's daughter comes to ask for his p[ay] and the boots.

On the 23rd V: came back from Versailles with the news that Lenormand was unwilling to make any further payments until the Martin attachments had been lifted.

On the 23rd, Robert asks to come to dinner by letter on Saturday the 26th.

On the 24th, Chapron announces 15 to play. Same day Mezange comes to say that the Coul: play has been turned down by the Francois and that he is going to take it to Audinot's, having first taken it to Louris.

On the 25th, many 2s were emphasised, I received a letter from Prosper that was full of them, etc....

On the 26th, a letter from my elder son asking if he can could come on the 28th. He had come on the 6th February and 50 days had elapsed from one visit to the next.

On the 28th, my eldest comes, he emphasises the number 15 by borrowing Voltaire's work on the Reign of Louis 15. He says that I should request a certificate of health and that with that, they could not refuse to let me out, although he says that this would harm his interests, and that on the question of marriage, they had said: the father is at Charenton, if it is because of madness we don't want the son, if it is because of a book, we don't care. He says nothing that is satisfactory and as usual, he tells me that I am still in lots of books.

On the 31st, the partner Robert appeared again, there was some play-acting. C. brought me down and announced a .... to me, I thought he was talking about me, but he was referring to someone else. The number 6 was emphasised.

April

On the 3rd, I perform a scene from The Deserter at the concert, firmly resolved not to sing any more even though I was warmly applauded.

On the 4th, C. told me that the doctor had not approved of my composing bits of verses and had made some very unpleasant remarks and threats on the matter.

On the 5th, Robert and his assistant come to see me but I do not receive them.

On the 6th, Descamps came to have coffee for the last time. It was therefore on the 7th that he was missing.

On the 8th, he was informed that he was expected, he refused and we saw that it was by order.

On the 9th, Chapron had not brought the newspaper for three days, we had invited him to come on the evening of the 8th, he had refused and had appeared to be avoiding us. The morning of that same day, Thieri brings me the letter that he has just received from the prefect of the département for his conscription. He goes to Paris.

On the 10th, everything becomes clear and it seemed that none of all this came from the master.

On the 13th, I had someone from Versailles with me, and Md. was in Paris. Between midday and one o'clock, C. sent for me and begged me not to say anything more to the Louvigni woman. He read me a letter that she had written and that had been intercepted in which that hussy said horrible things about me. B.... *of October.*

On the 15th, Md. came back from Paris having met with no success in the Martin affair. Normand had not been prepared to complete anything without Md.'s undertaking and we were to meet up in the week. What was most extraordinary about this was that J.... in his last letter had foretold misfortune for that day. He is therefore in the know and consequently treacherous. We fall out on that day.

On the 18th, Babeuf informed us that instead of being here for 6 months as Mr. de C. had at first told us, he was leaving in a week, which was false.

On the 19th, Daubac appeared dressed as a priest. This disguise surprised and displeased me. That morning, I had sent word to Versailles to get responses from Lenormand and in return for Trecour's. He was taking too long over this business and this both worried and vexed me. In the evening I received a letter from Jaillot about the person whom he had sent. Things *calmed down.*

On the 20th, Lenormand sends his 3rd payment via my express messenger.

On the 22nd, I receive the news that J and his V: want to come on the 26th and it seems that it's to make a scene.

On the 24th, C. shows me a letter from B the elder who does not want Moses to see his brother.

On the 25th, I receive a letter from J reassuring me about what I thought.

On the 26th after dinner, Md. leaves for Paris and is to return on the 28th.

On the same day a letter from Trecour saying that the business meeting of the 27th to which Md. has gone cannot take place because of the illness that has struck Lenormand down, which was a lie.

Note concerning my periods of detention

I was arrested in Paris at the hotel du Dannemark in my wife's apartment on the 17th February 1777 and taken to the dungeons of Vincennes where I remained in residence at No 11 until the 13th or 15th July 1778 when they came to fetch me to hear my case at the parliament of Aix. The case was thrown out and I was merely sentenced to be exiled from the city of Marseilles for three years, which meant that the whole affair lasted six years since it began in July 1772 and ended in July 1778, or nine years if the three years of exile from Marseilles are included. We left Aix again for Vincennes on the 13th July 1778, on the 15th I escaped from Valence and six week[s] later, that is on the 25th August, I was recaptured at La Coste where I had stupidly taken refuge, but lack of money had prevented me from doing anything else. Thus I was returned to the dungeons of Vincennes on the 7th September 1778 and placed in No 6 where I remained as well as in the Bastille and at Charenton until the 3rd April 1790, and so this first period of detention is 13 years 45 days.

I was rearrested on the 6th March 1801, after eleven years of freedom and this second period of detention including the Prefecture, Pelagie, B..., and Charenton has up until today, the 7th May 1808, lasted 7 years 62 days.

Up to today, the 7th May 1808, there has therefore been altogether a total period of detention of 20 years 3 months and 17 days.

I have never spoken of my ideas or of my opinions in my Diary but the determination with which they seem to have fixed the numbers 23 and 17 at all my different periods of detention leads me to believe that the 7th May 1808 so perfectly matches 23 and 17 that I must naturally entertain some hopes, and all the more so since it was in May that I was married, and since these numbers are those of my age and of the day of that sad period in my life with which my chains have been rightly soiled since it was then that they were forged, and I did the wrong thing as on so many other occasions.

Diary Continued

On the 27th, the number 2 is emphasised.

On the same day, Mr. Mezange comes to see me and talks to me of deaths.

On the 28th, Md. returns from Paris with a new young lady for me. My son also comes to dinner and strongly emphasises the 9 and the 7. There is talk of deaths and births. We go with my son to see M. de C. He returns the book about Louis 15.

On the 29th, ideas of death come to the fore all day long.

May 1808

Lenorman not having sent in on Sunday the first of the month, I sent off to Versailles the following day.

On the 2nd my express messenger brings me back my fourth month without letters. There is talk at J's of door to Versailles.

On the 4th, Milli Henriette and a young lady of her acquaintance came to dine with us unexpectedly. A little later, Asselin and his wife also came but did not dine. They came to tell me that Després was still asking for injunctions because of 50 or 60 francs costs. They babbled on at length about absurdities.

On the 5th, M. Roi, an ex-hotelier came to dine with us f[o]r the 1st time.

On the evening of the 7th, they told me they were sure that from 9 to 10 in the evening someone very often came up into my bedroom.

On the 8th, M. de Coul: gives me a 1-act play to examine; it seemed made for his name-day.

On the 9th, Claudine and the planned pieces are rehearsed for the first time, and on the morning of the 10th, I am told that, with the exception of Md. Quesnet's part, the two other women's parts are being changed, which gives a good idea of how many unexpected changes there were. There were other similar ideas throughout the day.

On the 11th, nothing.

On the 13th, I receive a letter dated the 10th from Trecour containing one from Lenormand dated the 1st, and all of this is just a pretence of delays that does not fool me. I immediately write to all the business people to send back Md. Quesnet's securities which these people tell her they need, which is just a joke.

On the morning of the 14th, I reflect that, quite apart from the revolting absurdity of the system of numbers that dull imbeciles are using against me, it also has the disadvantage of making me everywhere into an object of derision that can seemingly be mocked with impunity, a major disadvantage that my children should never have had to suffer. Besides, it is a small victory of stupidity over intelligence, that is all they have so they are welcome to it.

On the 14th, I receive a package from Courtois containing his accounts and a bill of exchange for 600 [fr.] 20 days after sight. C. honours it and says that it is by an oversight.

On the 15th in the morning a command from Robin to make immediate payment of the sum of 1000 [fr.] due to him by a deed executed at Finot the notary's at Charenton and which he transmitted to M. Leroux, ex-police sergeant at Versailles, in the rue de Noailles to whom I am writing.

On the 17th Moses and Md. go to see the D. de

V...

On the 18th in the morning I receive a letter from the doctor promising to send his virgin again on the 21st. I write at once to prevent this and write to my elder son to come and see me on Saturday the 21st, the day when I am to expect this visit.

On the evening of the 20th, I receive a letter from Trecour naming the 21st at 3 o'clock for the meeting with Lenormand and inviting Md. to be present. She does indeed leave that day for Paris. On the other hand, noted that Jail: absolutely wanted to send his V... that day, all this was therefore arranged.

On the 21st, Md. leaves for Paris at eleven o'clock. That same day, the woman above my head goes. I ask for her room and am refused. J's wife does not come.

My elder son comes, I ask to be allowed to go for a walk with him in the island. C. makes all kinds of difficulties and all sorts of unpleasant remarks to my son about me; there is no one more stupid or more indecent. He says that the Emperor has pronounced that I should be kept locked up for life, for the simple reason that I had requested to be let out. In the end, he allows me to go into the island, telling my son that he is responsible for me. During my conversation with my son, my son says that the rumours caused by the book were starting to subside, but that it was still being sold for 300 [fr.] which makes a superb 13 and 9.

Md. comes back from Paris on the 23rd. She brings back L's necessities, L. and the 600 [fr.]. She has not yet been able to do anything with Lenormand because the papers have not arrived. In the morning, I learn that C. has again made many nasty remarks about Moses in front of everyone.

On the 25th, as we had remarked that M. de C. was behaving oddly towards us, Md. went downstairs on the pretext of paying her board and lodging and learned from him that the police were claiming that I had appended libellous verses to the plays composed for his name-day, which is false. He let it be known that there would be another search and in general, since he was spreading such bad rumours about me in his house, you could bet that I could expect something unpleasant. He said that they were going to report on the papers taken from me and that until then I must not leave the house, and that consequently I should ask nothing from him. He refused me any change of room. I wrote to him about all this on the morning of the 26th.

They say that on that morning, Leon had tried to run away from the parish. They met up with him at Alfort. Md and I were still worried about all this. It was clear that C. was changing his attitude to me.

On the 31st, my younger son paid a suprise visit and told me that he had come to ask my consent to marry Mlle de S. d'Aig: I strongly approved of this arrangement and we needed to go to the notary's to sign. C. refused to let me go, the notary came himself and told C. that for such a matter, I absolutely must go to his offices. Eventually, C. agreed provided it was in the evening at half past 8. While we waited, we drew up the deed, when a letter arrived by express messenger from my elder son, requesting an hour's audience the following day. I replied that I would expect him and we continued to draw up our deed when suddenly my elder son himself arrived. I went outside with him to speak privately with him, whereupon he informed me that a trap was being laid for me and that just as soon as this marriage that his brother spoke of was accomplished I would be removed from here and put in an awful fortress such as the Tower of Ham or the Mont St Michel. I went back upstairs and immediately told my younger son that I would not sign anything, and that he should come back the next day. He left, and before his departure, my elder son assured me that he would see to it that nothing happened to me.

June 1808

The 1st: the younger son came back to get me to go and sign. I gave him the attached conditions. He went off saying that he would tell his new relations this and he took note of them, but expostulating greatly about the wickedness and lies of his brother. He promised to let me have news when there was some. The elder son, too, had said that he was going to marry.

On the morning of the 2nd, they came to tell me that the house was no longer able to give either sugar or coffee.

On the 2nd, the wigmaker brings me back *his promissory note* with a request for me to write him another.

On the 1st, the newspaper is missing.

On the 2nd, the elder son comes back and reassures me concerning all my fears of the previous day. He says he is leaving for Echafour and is in a great hurry, wanting to arrive there before his brother. On the 2nd, Md. receives her papers from Chartres.

Right from the 1st of the month, the results of the scene of the previous day had made Md. Q.. poorly. The fever began that very day, the next day she was better, but on the third the fever returned preceded by a fainting-fit and vomiting. The surgeon believed that this fever would be intermittent in character. She was advised to go on a starvation diet and to take four flower infusion with honey because she had a violent cough. On the 4th, she felt a little better but had no appetite.

On the 4th, I received a letter from the elder son. On the same day, Md. still had fever and was coughing a great deal. She was still starving herself and in the evening, her headaches increased very much. She had vomited again in the morning but the night was quiet. That same day, Varen: emphasised the number 8 from the morning on.

On the 5th, Mad. still had fever from one o'clock to 5 and even some lightheadedness. In the evening, she continued to complain greatly of headaches, but the night and in general all her nights are fairly quiet.

On the morning of the 6th, the American woman withdrew and Milli Lépinai who had come the day before came in to nurse her. The attack which usually occurred at one o'clock did not happen until a quarter past three, it was milder in character, there was no hallucinating and the patient did not suffer so much with headaches. The fits of coughing caused by the fever were less severe, the patient drank a lot as usual, having only had beef-tea in the morning. The night was quiet.

On the 7th, she took some ipecacuanha in manna.[22] The fever came on at 4 o'clock and lasted until eleven. The attack of fever was very violent but in the evening, the headaches were less violent, the patient took a remedy the results of which did not bring with them any bad symptoms, and the night was quiet as usual.

On the morning of the 8th, two letters came first thing, one from Md. Monchinat, the other from my son announcing his visit the following day, the 9th.

The fever was delayed by two hours, it had come on at four the previous day. It did take 8 until six. Its character was more or less the same, however, the patient said that she had suffered a little less and that it was her thighs now that were hurting. In the evening, her thoughts were a little rambling. The night passed well, the fever having left her around midnight, and the next day the surgeon told me that he hoped that it would not be long now and that although the fever was inflammatory, he saw no danger in this.

On the 9th, the attack came at the same hour as the previous day but it was less violent and the patient suffered less. The same diet was observed and the doctor found her improved. The fever left her around midnight.

That same day, my elder son came to see me and saw Md. also. He seemed less keen to complete our business and said that he thought we could go and sign our deed in Paris. In the evening, I received 2 letters from Arles and the promise of 1300 [fr.].

On the 10th, the attack came even later and did not occur until half past seven. The attack was absolutely identical to that of the previous night and the fever did not cease until nearly morning which in some ways made this attack longer than the previous one. However, she rested and appeared calm but extremely weak towards morning.

Memories

I must not forget that in the first eight days of her illness, my dear friend said some very harsh and heart-rending things to me which, as soon as I found myself alone, made me shed many tears. One day, she said to me as if to thank me for my pains: *So you really do want me to live?* Another time: *You won't have me for long*, words all the more terrible in that they chimed with those of my dream 12 or 13 months ago. Another day she said to me with a fixed stare: *I knew that you would bury me* (oh! no no, for I should follow you).

Diary continued

On the 11th, the convulsions did not occur but around nine o'clock the fever took hold, the patient had it all night, spending it in great agitation, but there were definite signs of improvement.

On the morning of that same day, I received a letter for Mlle Finance and ....

On the 12th, the day was quiet, much weakness but no fever, the patient had had it in the night of the 11th to the 12th but it had left her around six o'clock in the morning. At eleven o'clock in the evening on the 12th, the fever had not yet appeared but from nine to eleven there had been some mild symptoms of minor convulsions. The night of the 12th to the 13th was a little restless.

On the 13th, weakness without fever, the night of the 13th to the 14th quiet, the treatment changed on the 14th. The doctor prescribed lemonade with cream of tartar, no more than 3 enemas instead of 4, and chicken broth and a little vermicelli in beef-tea as before.

On the morning of the 14th, however, the patient said that she had had a little fever during the night. That day she was prescribed lemonade with cream of tartar. All day long on the 14th the patient was weak, sad and anxious. She continued with her enemas the effects of which continued to be astonishing.

On the evening of the 14th, an officer from Breslau came to bring her a dress sent by L.L. She seemed almost insensible such was her state of depression. The night of the 14th to the 15th was bad, the patient had the fever again though less severely, she was anxious and continued to be distressed. She had coughed a great deal during the night which I attributed to the cream of tartar and I stopped her taking it. The night of the 15th to the 16th was good and the patient experienced only a slight attack of fever during the night.

On the 15th, she had taken the air for a short while and had eaten two bowls of soup. On the night of the 15th to the 16th, the patient was still a little feverish and was very restless during the night.

On the evening of the 16th, I received a letter

from Jaillot.

The night of the 16th to the 17th also restless and still a little fever.

The night of the 17th to the 18th was good, there was just a little disturbance.

The night of the 19th to the 20th very restless and the fever lasted six hours. The 19th during the day was not good, the patient spent it in a state of dreadful depression. On the 18th she received a visit from M. Vautrain and on the 19th from Mlle Flore's sister who informed her of the sister's death. She wept and I think that these two visits upset her much too much.

The night of the 19th to the 20th had been good.

On the morning of the 20th, my elder son came to say that his brother had tricked me out of the contractual conditions and that he was still going ahead, that he too had a marriage in prospect procured by Md. de Sauran et de Talaru, a girl with 5 thousand *livres* income. In accordance with my purposes, he was going to work for the surrender of my papers.

On the same day, the 20th, the churchwardens came to give me two pieces of blessed bread, Varennes accompanied them and by my order gave or rather said that we should give 30 s. That same day, the 20th, people talk to me of deaths a great deal.

The night of the 20th to the 21st was good although she had been very worried during the day by the bill from Diart which arrived on the 20th.

On the 21st, my elder son came back and told me that he had been very pleased with B. S. at the police and that part of my papers would be returned to him.

On the 22nd, the patient took medecine. She had been well all day and all evening, but the night was not quite as good as the previous ones. The medicine worked wonders. The 22nd was very good too but the night of the 23rd to the 24th, the patient had much fever preceded by shivering as in the first attacks. The

24th was fairly quiet but the patient was so weak that she felt ill in the afternoon. However, the night of the 24th to the 25th went well and she took her medecine in the morning on the 25th. It was Mme Laine who cared for her that day, her usual nurse having been obliged to absent herself for two days.

The 25th passed quite well but the fever took hold again in the night of the 25th to the 26th and the doctor seemed determined to break it with quinine. On the 25th, I won 61fr. 10 s on the lottery.

The day of the 26th went fairly well except for much weakness which did not, however, prevent the patient from walking right round the garden. The night had gone well but a sort of rash came out.

On the morning of the 27th, my express messenger from Versailles returned without bringing back the monthly payment. He had been told to come back next Sunday.

On the morning of the 27th, he caused a row with Thierri and stopped him going to Charenton.

On the evening of the same day, M. de Coul: came to see Md. Quesnet. The night of the 27th to the 28th was again marked by an attack of fever. On the morning of the 28th, the patient took three bowls of quinine and vomited them 2 hours later. She was very weak all day long. In the evening, she took more of it in water and threw it up again half an hour later.

That day, Th: was in Paris and saw someone who spoke to him of my affairs with exactly the same understanding as me: see my notes on the sum of my detentions.

The night of the 28th to the 29th went well and in the morning the patient took a quinine enema and a tincture in a potion. Md. Populus comes on the evening of the 28th and promises to stay.

The night of the 29th to the 30th passed without fever and it was day

On the 30th, the patient is well. Robert and the priest come to see her. M. Daligre and Dumon came too.

The night of the 30th to the 1st passed very well and the patient took quinine on the 1st July in the morning.

Month of July

On the 1st, following my reflections the previous evening at M. de C.'s, everything that was obstructing the theatre was brought down and they came to ask me for the key to lock it and this was brought back to me immediately.

On the 2nd, M. Roi, at my entreaty but on a day chosen by him, came to dine with us and agreed to come to help me at meetings with my creditors. The same storm was experienced in Paris.

Since she has now missed two attacks of fever and is in convalescence, we will keep up with the quinine but not with the health report.

On the second, I waited for the p: de Jai: who had threatened the 2nd or the 3rd but she did not come on the 2nd.

On the 3rd, I sent off to Versailles for the second time, but the express messenger returned without bringing anything back. Two letters, one by express messenger, the other by post said that the attachments stopped the payments and one of these letters announced a visit from Lenormand at the end of the week.

On the evening of the 4th, idea Ø, the 82nd.

That same day nineteen is emphasised all day long.

On the 5th, the elder son came and proposed that we immediately complete our business together; we postponed this till the next day. He promised to come and bring my papers. He continued with the same ideas about his brother that he had expressed.

In the evening, M. de C. made his 3rd visit to Md:

On the 6th, we expected Md. St. Aubin who had promised to come. She came, was very amiable and saw M. de C.

On the 7th, my son writes to say that he cannot come but that his trip will be brief and that on his return he will bring the papers. L.L.'s young friend comes back for the 3rd time on the 6th.

On the 8th, my elder son sent two letters still relating to affairs of interest. In the evening, I saw C with whom I was very pleased.

On the 9th, I expected Lenormand, Diart and M. roi. They came, Diart appeared to consent to my proposals but he asked for five days' reflection and deferred with these two gentlemen till the 15th. As for Lenormand, he still refused to pay his month's rent until Diart was accommodated, and he promised also to come *on the 15th*. Lots of farcical talk from M. Roi. In the evening, I paid a surprise visit to the pottery.

On the morning of the 10th, a little farce from Alexandre and a long one from Populus. On the same day, Leveque says goodbye and Md. makes a joke of breaking a bottle of wine.

Diart writes to say that he will not come to terms. M. de Savine leaves on the *11th July 1808.*

On the 12th, 4 women come to see Md., but I don't see them.

In the evening, we are notified that Després is putting pressure on for the library.

On the 13th, I instructed Fleurot to see all my creditors and to settle everything with them.

On the 14th, my son came as he had said he would. He seemed as if he was managing things more positively, promised the papers very soon. We went walking together etc.......

On the 16th, dismissal of Maniard, a lot of commotion to get another, bad behaviour on the part of C.. in this respect. I tell him that I am going to ask to be transferred.

On the 17th, I sent him Maniard's money in a letter, he sent it back to me insolently with a note as stupid and as dull as he is. He held fast that he would only give me Maniard or nobody. On the 17th, Robert and one of his friends come.

On the 18th, I received a letter from my son relating to the papers.

On the 20th, my son came to fix a day for the surrender of the papers. He said that the one he would have chosen would have been Friday, that is, in 3 days, but following representations by Md. P, he had decided to go with her on Thursday, the 21st, and he said that he would come back to dine with me on Thursday the 28th.

In the evening of the 26th, M.C. called me down to communicate to me a letter from the Prefect who was most displeased with the whole business of the police superintendant, saying that it was possible that these people were trying to take me away and, finally, that he forbade me to be let out any more, and that I must not set foot outside the hospice.

On the 27th, a young 13-year-old girl came with M. Lepinai and all day long, the *villain* was emphasised.

In the evening, a row with C. regarding the rehearsal.

On the 28th, the elder son came as always.

On the 30th, J: had threatened his V: She did not come.

On the 31st, Md. St. Aubin gave me 2 white turkey-cocks which she brought to me herself.

August 1808

On the 1st, Leon is refused admittance. The same day, Md. comes back from Paris.

On the 2nd, the elder son came; he said that owing to my entry on the list, I was considered banned. He took the outlines of the plan to finish it with me. La P. came back from Paris and said that there was nothing to fear with regard to the transfer and that my papers would be returned to me *in a fortnight*.

In the night of the 2nd to the 3rd, a great din above my head.

On the 3rd, the younger son came at my request and asked me if I would sign his contract of marriage. I said yes and did so. We were reconciled with each other and he promised to finish soon, he asked for two months, and promised meanwhile to pay a call on Normand and also to do something about the library.

He had scarcely gone out when the elder son arrived. He had his lease all ready and presented it to me. I asked him for a few days to think it over, he agreed reluctantly, he would have preferred to deal with it straightaway. It seems that both of them were leaving for Echafour the following day.

On the 6th, the younger son came back and things went marvellously well. He had barely arrived when M. Trecour arrived; it was his 2nd visit. My son left that afternoon and we spoke a great deal of business matters with M. Trecour. 26 was emphasised.

The elder son came back on the 10th and made a 17. He had come to get my answer on the lease and I gave it back to him with my objections. He took it away and promised to come back on the 15th to say his goodbyes to me. He was going back to the army, planning not to return for a long time if he could not come to terms with me.

On the 13th, we celebrated Md. Q:'s name-day very gaily. Everyone joined in most obligingly.

On the 15th, M. de C. informed me that the play

which was to be performed on the 18th would be postponed until the 23rd.

That same day, Md. is still suffering from something; she has a serious attack of diarrhoea.

On the 16th, Md. de Vion, M.C.'s niece, arrives.

On the evening of the 18th, I receive 300 [fr.] from Courtois.

On the 20th, I expected Md. de Soran, she did not come. In the evening, I went to ask M.C. to go with Md. to Nogent the next day, but he absolutely refused to do so. He agreed that my detention was by the government, but through the family, he believed that the children would do something in the end etc. etc.....

On the 25th, Md. de Soran came for the 2nd time. She spoke to me of the younger son's marriage, approved of the fact that I had given my consent, said that the elder son was a scatter-brain, told me not to worry about the future, that I could not fail to get 4000 [fr.] and that Md. Q. would not be abandoned; saw C. twice, asked him for access to the island, was refused, preached to me a lot.

THE FOURTH NOTEBOOK: 18 JULY to (30 NOVEMBER) 1814

July

On the 18th July 1814, Armand came to make his 10th visit as he had announced. It was similar to the letter that announced this visit, saying that Mr Lacroix was no longer anything at the Ministry, that he had been replaced by a Mr Biset, that this Mr Biset had told him that he did not know M. de Sade, that he would look into his case and that in two or three months he would be able to tell him whether it was possible to take *the air*; that he, Armand, was going to Echaufour for 2 months at least, and 3 at the most, and that in accordance with the period of time laid down by M. Biset, he would act and believed he would then obtain a result. This response put me into quite a mood. I pointed out to him how contradictory it was but nothing could shake him. He charged Md. Quesnet to see the Director and to ask him for permission to take the air, saying that this wish was consistent with his own (Armand's) and that he authorised him to make this request. I begged him at least to put the summer months back on the same footing as the winter months, which amounted to 3 days per month, he refused in the harshest fashion. For the rest, the visit was very sad and he said that if he was still in Paris on Friday, he would come to say goodbye to me. On that day, Armand emphasises 2 and 3 and 9.

On the 19th, Coulmier appears at the House.

On the same day, Md. saw the new director and asked him for her new bedroom and for permission to take the air. She obtains the bedchamber but as to taking the air, the decision is postponed until the ruling which, the director says, will be made within two months. This agrees with what Armand has said.

On the 20th, Md. pays a quick visit to Paris.

Magdeleine Leclerc

On the 21st, Mgl: came to make her 57th and 81st in all; I had warned her that Annette would knock once to bring the newspaper; she came, and Mgl. was quite affected, she almost did not recover, and on the whole was cold during the entire ø which had just begun in a desultory fashion. She said she knew Lefebvre by sight but had not spoken to him and assured me that she would not speak to him. She promised to return on either the 23rd or the 28th, and I urged her to prefer the 28th because there was a trip to Paris. She told me that if she did not appear at 8 o'clock on the 23rd, she would not come until the 28th. She asked for a franc on top of the 4 which I gave her on account upon her first visit, which made 5 for her. She said that the Santeuil woman asked her and her mother lots of questions about the places she went, both outside the house and inside. She confessed that she had taken the key and said that she would bring it back, but said nothing further about the scissors that she was to have sharpened.

Same day a little later, the mother came and I was very happy with her. She told me that S. has paid her and that Mgl. has worked there for 19 days.

On the 21st, Md. changes rooms.

On the 22nd, Armand does not come, proving that he has left on that day or the day before after his 9th visit.

July Note

It is on the 23rd August 1812 that Md. receives her first wages of 300 [fr.].

On the 26th, 2 is emphasised.

On the 28th, Mgl. comes to do her 82nd and 58th bedroom, is very kind, even makes arrangements for the change of house so that she can still be near me, says that she thinks that all this will go better than I think, says that they found out about the pâté, forbids the breakfasts, receives only one franc, and says that she will send word tomorrow to find out if I have received it, but says this to please me, asks me for the 2 or 3 from Grasville, brings back two pairs of stockings. She sets a date for August 6th.

On the 27th, Md. goes to Paris to see B.S. and Pal: She is displeased with the former and pleased with the latter. In agreement with the people she has seen, she prescribes a course of conduct for me which I am going to observe. As regards Boursier, he agrees to advance the 1st month only. Paquet comes on that day and says that the work has been found good, but that circumstances etc...... he has lodged it with Testu and will come and deliver a response to me without fail on Thursday 4th or Thursday 11th.

On the 29th Coulmiers comes.

On the 30th la Coul: who was supposed to come the day before comes to fetch the two volumes etc.... etc.....

By the 30th I had had my 4th sleepless night.

On the 2nd Mezange pays a surprise visit at dinner. At first, he did not want to stay; he promised to take action with regard to the Le Cl:

On the 2nd Quenet sees Bechet in Paris who tells him that he will come and see me but that he cannot undertake anything until January.

On the 3rd the Santeuil woman comes to visit me.

On the 6th, Mgl. came to make her 83rd and her 59th. She starts off in Santeuil's rooms where she has breakfast, and does not reach me until half past nine, and stays for only an hour and a half, that is, she leaves at eleven o'clock, still very pleased. She dispels all my anxieties and promises to come back on Friday the 12th. She says that she will take Madame a bouquet on the eve of the feast of the Blessed Virgin.

On the 9th Coulmier appears at the house.

On the 10th I sent a request to Md. Leclerc to come and see me about her own affairs, and she said that she could not.

In the afternoon, I went down to meet her and found her taking a woman to the governor. I told her that I would wait for her. I waited for her for a good hour and she made a show of disappearing in another direction. I went back down and asked for her and was told she was in the hall. So she had disappeared without my seeing her. I sent a message for her to come and have a word with me. The answer came back straightaway that she was not there any more but that she was with Bernard. I went down there and she had not set foot there. Finally, it became clear that she was playing games with me and also with herself for Dumoustier was not at home.

Madame had also thrown a temper tantrum which obliged me to send for her at her children's. She and her servant had disturbed my Midday nap twice, it was obvious that it was a day of practical jokes. Md. came back but I was unable to see the Leclerc girl again and all this seemed most extraordinary to me. Magd. said that she knew nothing about this but that it was likely that her mother had gone up the kitchen stairs.

On the 12th, Mgl. came as promised. I was quite ill which she noticed and appeared to show concern, saying that she was unwell too, had a chill, said that her mother did not wish to do anything about the position until she was sure that I was free, promised to come back on Saturday the 20th. Moreover I was quite pleased with this, she put my mind at rest, told me not to worry, that she would not go to the ball with her friends, as she had said she would at first. In addition, she babbled on at length, telling ridiculous tales, like the one about her mother not wanting to commit herself to anything until I was free. She said that Varenne was going to marry the Dufour woman and that a grand dinner was being given for this, etc... etc... She stayed only an hour with me. Bernard came to knock for the second time to query some copying and interrupted us which displeased her all the more.

Mgl. said that if her mother did not wish it, she could not do it, not yet being of an age to do her own will, but that her mother would like it; which means that her mother will put conditions on her visits.

Reflect about all this, very essential to reread.

It is clear that Mgl's attachment would be subordinated to her mother's advice, and that if her mother did not agree to let me have her, she would not come, that on the other hand, the mother who was loudly proclaiming that she did not wish to make any arrangement nor would she allow anything to be arranged unless I get out, would not agree to anything without terms, that her terms would be all the harsher given that this woman had money, that she had no need of me, and that she would perhaps demand *with threats* things that I could not accept, which means that the girl would not come; that in a word, this mother's self-interest carried more weight than the girl's interest in me, and that all this was my fault and would not have happened if I had been less eager, and if I had hidden my feelings better.

This lack of interest that Mgl. is affecting, it is as if she is saying: *Oh, lord, don't go to so much trouble for me, monsieur, for you shall never have me*. Add to this the certainty that you must have that she comes to see you only as a *telegraph* and you will have sure proof that you are nothing but a dupe in all of this.[23]

As far as her kindnesses are concerned, the fact is that she has been told: agree to everything in order to win his confidence, otherwise he will not want to receive you any more, and our plan has failed. In a word, they have made this girl into one of those female spies that are sent to get close to condemned men to try to discover their secrets. Examine carefully her coldness, her insouciance in pleasure and in conversations, and in these you will see irrefutable proof of what I am suggesting, and it is since she began visiting that she has behaved in this way for when she was a child there was more truth and more honesty in her.

On the 13th, I receive a letter from Armand which has been in transit for 9 days. This letter is most absurd and full of farcical nonsense.

On the 13th I met the Lecl: woman who told me that she would come on Wednesday the 17th.

On the 14th, Mgl. brought Md. Quesnet a potted jasmine.

On the 16th, a grand dinner, they say, for the whole management to decide on the rules, and they add that this dinner is to be repeated on Thursday the 18th and Sunday the 21st.

On the 17th, the Leclerc woman came at my request, and destroyed quite naturally everything that I had believed and written about her previously. She still seemed very resolved to let me have her daughter under no other conditions than those which I had set myself and which she could not argue with. She said that her daughter did not go bathing, that as regards the bad company that I scolded her for keeping, she could not stop her daughter from working with those girls, but that she did not see them. But one thing that pleased me was that she said that her daughter would still come with me even if I did not manage to find a position for her herself. When I mentioned a position in the theatres to her, she found the money inconsiderable and said that she would wait here until I had found something better for her, and on the whole, she was still determined that neither she nor her daughter should move until I was out.

On the 18th Paquet comes and takes Md. de Saxe away. The Calias woman is a surprise guest at dinner, there are six of us at table.

On the 19th Md. goes to Paris. She is to spend the night there, she is going to get money. Before leaving, Mad: speaks to me like an angel about Mgl. She seemed to want not to be a great nuisance...

On the 19th Magd., called by me as she came out of the Santeuil woman's room where I did not know she was, came for a moment and was very sullen.

The next day, the 20th, she came to make her 85th visit in all, that is, her 61st in the bedchamber and her 85th overall. She stayed for more than two hours, had breakfast and was very amiable. She told me that the following day, she was going with her sister and another young lady of the same situation as her sister, destroyed all my anxieties and my suspicions and promised to come back on Friday the 26th of this month.

Md. comes back from Paris on the 21st. She has seen Vaillant who has told her that many things have been written against me, among other things that I had been seducing people for two weeks, that I must obtain a certificate of life and morals to counter all this, that in addition, my petition to the police had been directed to Master Denon, saying that they were going to write to my son about all this, which led Madame to expect that I was going to be let out, and that they should consequently make arrangements. She said that all this had been written on the 17th.

As for Boursier, he gave only the 153 francs and promised to give the rest on the 2nd September, that is, in 13 days or 2 weeks, which forms the number 227 so often seen in the numerical system. He had also put off the question of Madame's living expenses until the same time. Md. says that he was sure that I would not stay here but that it was possible also that I would be sent elsewhere.

On the 24th I was advised that mother Leclerc was coming the next day, the 25th, at one o'clock. Md. Leclerc came and as she was in a hurry, she promised to come back the following day. It is an interruption.

I wait for Mgl: on the morning of the 26th, she came but was very cold. She stayed for two hours, apologised for her coldness which she said was due to her health not being good. She promised to return on Friday the 2nd of September and did not want anything for breakfast on that day.

On the 26th August 1814, Guerignon and Bernard are forbidden to speak to me and to read my newspaper, and I forecast that this proves Mgl's latest and that these are the reasons for her coldness.

I waited for Md. Lec.... she came and told me that Stanislas had seen Mgl. come in and shut herself in with me, and that she did not know what would come of all this, but she did not seem to have cooled and promised to let me know the outcome. I went to see the Santeuil woman to whom I spoke only about the business of the newspaper. She said to me that things would perhaps work out better than I thought, that she would enquire about the situation and would tell me what she had learned about it.

On the same day, Md. saw the governor who seemed very harsh to her, and who said that he had very strict orders concerning me. However, he agreed that until he had taken advice, Guerignon could come back to read, and in the morning he had agreed that Bernard might continue his copying, and I surmised from all of this that everything was going as it has in the past, that is, that a little slap was being administered for the form and to play a joke, which at bottom was no great harm, as will be shown by what follows.

On the 27th, I learnt that Dubuisson and Dumoustier had seized the script of The Mysterious Tower from the copyist; I had given him this for fair-copying with the promise to let him have it back.[24]

On the 28th, Cueno reappears and says that he will come back on Tuesday or Friday.

On the 29th, Madame goes to Paris to see the fair and promises also to see Boursier for the 6 louis.

On the same day, Guerignon cannot come to read my newspaper any more, and all this heralds many new troubles for me.

On the 30th, Mad. came back from Paris and brought back the 3 louis. She had given the two Ganges volumes to Boursier, she had seen Vaillant who had seen a man high up who had seemed less strict than the other one, but who had asked the stupid and ridiculous question as to whether I was still mad, given that you had to be to have written the book attributed to me. From what Mad. was saying, he had said that 3 police superintendents would be coming to inform themselves of my conduct, and as a consequence, I was strongly advised to behave myself until then. But as there was a clear contradiction in all this, I fear that all this is just a farce.

Month of September 1814

On the 1st, Md. told me that she had been told that the ruling[25] would be announced in two weeks time.

On the 2nd, Mgl. came to make her 88th in total and her 64th in the bedchamber. It was easy to see that she had been ill, she was feeling the effects, she had trimmed the h: of her c:.[26] Someone came and knocked at the door which disturbed us. It hurt her. A little later, she talked of going away and promised to return on Friday the 9th. She stayed for barely one and a half hours. She wanted chocolate for the first time. It is noticeable that she showed a great preference for the Santeuil woman over Madame.

On the 2nd, Dumoustier came to return the Mysterious Tower to me, advising me in a whisper to have no communication with the patients under pain of losing my walks. I replied to him that this was indeed my plan but that I did not want any threats.

On the 7th, Coulmier dines at the house and sees us.

On the 9th, Mgl. made her 89th in total. I was warned that she was to be absent for 9 days by 9 peaches. She behaved very well, stayed for two and a half hours, and promised me that she would come and see me again on the day of our name-day and on routine visit on the 17th. She said she would give me rabbit-skin stockings for my name-day.

On the 17th, Mgl. comes to make her 89th in total[27]. She says that if am not within the rules,[28] we will have no means of seeing each other again. For the rest, very amiable and I have never been more pleased with her. She took away Le Portier des C.[29] and is very attentive, passionate, etc....... She asked whether or not Hélène was Moses's daughter, complained about a remark made by Deslande the father, gave me the idea of a chamber for our meals.

Md. left on the 16th to get money, came back with it and said that Boursier was out in the country for 8 to 10 days and that it was the 2nd clerk who had paid it. As for Vaillant, he said that Armand's name had been called to appear at the police regarding me, that he had presented himself 10 days ago and that he did not know the results.

On the 19th, Varene reappears after 13 days'

absence.

On the 23rd, Md. Lec. required for the 21st came, and I was very pleased with her.

On the 25th, Mgl's 90ieth. She came to breakfast but was quite ill, asked for 3 francs, made many promises for the future, destroyed everything that I had been told about her, promised to return on the 2nd October and said that she was too sick to go to the ball. I thought I saw truth in her suffering, but it is nonetheless true that the whole character of this visit suggested it was the last. She made me great promises of submissiveness and fidelity, promised that she would never go with anyone that I might not like or that might give me cause for concern, appeared to fear another search of papers, etc......

Note for me. The newspapers of the 15th begin on the 28th September 1813.

On the 29th in the morning Helene gives Moses the best of news and says that she has the best information about it. Paquet came and had nothing further of advantage to say about the books. When I went for a walk with him, I met Md. Lec... who was cold almost to the point of impertinence. She approved of her daughter with regard to everything and did not even thank me for what I had given her for the name-day. Pointing out Paquet to her, I told her that he was now the one that I was employing for the position, and she received this information in the coolest of manners. From the reports that have reached me it seemed that it was very true that Mgl. had been at all the balls and had danced a great deal at them.

On the 30th September they came to have me sign the authorisation for the sale of the Saumane wood amounting to 800 francs.

Month of October 1814

On the 2nd at the time when I was expecting Mgl., she sent the Coulange woman with a letter saying that she could not come until next Sunday and she was sending me a good pair of nice warm stockings. I replied a little angrily.

On the 5th Md. makes a quick trip to Paris for the letter from M. Rose of Lille.

On the same day, Md. de Santeuil comes to read the newspaper to me for the first time.

It was on the 5th October that Md. sent off Maitre Roze's authorisation.

On the 9th, Mgl. made her 91st in all. She was very nice and said some very sensible things. She strongly urged me not to worry as far as she was concerned, assuring me that she would never fail me, that even if her mother did not leave the house, this would not prevent her from coming with me. She urged me not to spend money on her, saying that in the past I spent much less on her and that even so I was bothered by this and that it was right that it should bother me in quite a different way today, and said that she would give me another p. of rabbit-skin stockings for New Year's Day, and that when we were together, she would give me all sorts of things that could prove useful to me. She added that she was very badly fed, that only 3 francs were spent on her a week plus something extra for bedlinen, which, she told me very sweetly, meant that she did not now wish to eat good things that she would miss later. I gave her a little lesson in reading and writing, and she promised to spend time on this during the long evenings. But otherwise, I found that things were not going badly. She said that her health continues not to be good and that in 8 or 10 days she will consult De Guise if it continues to be poor.

On the 10th, Mezange paid a surprise visit and emphasised the word *bad news*.

On the 13th, Madame strongly emphasised

change and surprise.

On the 14th, Md. who had rowed with Annette the day before throws her out on the 14th. She had entered the house on the 15th, the year expired on the 14th, and so she has been here for one year only.

On the 15th, the new girl appears and promises to return the next day.

The governor writes to Armand and sends a message to Md. to check his address.

On the 16th, Mgl: who was supposed to be coming sends the Coulange woman with a letter to say that she will come in a week's time, that is, on the 23rd. Coulange had told me that what was preventing Mag. from coming was that she was working at the Blenie woman's. This was not true, she had been out walking with her mother.

On the 17th, Md. leaves for Paris and is not to return until the following day. Extraordinary remarks she made to me when she came to say goodbye, ridiculous remarks. She is taking away The Mysterious Tower and The Twins to sell them.

Md. came back from Paris on the 18th at dinner-time. She had lodged the two plays, one at the Odeon, the other at Fedeau. But she had seen Vaillant who had told her that the police had written to my family to take me away and that they had replied that they did not want this and that it was M. Cole, secretary of the police chief who had written and to whom a reply had been sent that the family did not want this. Apart from this, she was bringing back the month's rent with the money for the wood and said that Boursier will come and see me towards the end of the month.

On the same day, Md. Leclerc who was supposed to be coming on Friday the 21st sent word to say that she would not be coming until the 24th.

On the 20th, Mlle Montfort leaves the house to get married.

On the 23rd, I was expecting her (Magdeleine) at the usual hour, and at 10 o'clock the Coulange woman came to tell me that she would not be coming until eleven o'clock or midday. She came at quarter past twelve and stayed until 2 o'clock, still cold and when I reproached her for this, she said to me that it was the house that caused this and that she would be quite different outside. She made me a firm promise that she would remain faithful and devoted to me and that I could count on her; she had her period, and she produced the best possible arguments why it was not possible to have breakfast with me each time, arguments which I accepted. Throughout all this, spouted absurdities at length and even suggested that perhaps the ruling would not get me out, and that she would be confined, that we really should consider this. She took 10 [francs] for a new waistcoat which she undertook to buy, as well as two pairs of stockings. After all, there was some ø for a moment and promise of more next Sunday. She argued brilliantly about those mistresses or lovers who published the favours that they received and assured me that she had never committed any indiscretion of this kind.

On the 24th, I expected the mother who had promised to come and who did not come. But it was not her fault. On the same day, things were stolen from Quesnet's rooms and the two servants were suspected.

On the 26th, having given advance notice of her visit, the mother came at one o'clock and promises with an air of frankness and truth that none of our plans would be changed. She asked how I would go about things and I explained everything to her. With regard to M... she asked me if I had spoken about this to her daughter, I told her I had, she asked me what she had replied, in the affirmative, I answered. Oh well, she said, how could I not consent in view of that? She expressed the keenest wish to see her daughter happy and said that as far as this was concerned, she would much prefer to have her serve me simply than in other ways. I said all one can say on this matter and was pleased with the outcome. She told me that she thought Varenne was more stupid than smart and wicked, etc...... They say that the ruling has arrived.

On the 30th, Mgl. came, as she had promised, to make her 93rd visit. She stayed for two hours, arriving at 8 and not leaving until after 10. She was very amiable, promised to take great care of me once we were together, she drank, wrote and sang. She said that she was going to be better fed and that she was very pleased with her mother, that she was taking eau de Cologne and sugar in the evenings for her stomach and that it was doing her good. She seemed to be in amazing health. She had brought me a pair of stockings, etc....

On the 31st, I give up thinking that it will be the 1st November and favour the 31st December 1814. They say that the ruling will arrive in great detail and that one will not learn of one's fate for a week, the said ruling not taking effect until the 8th or the 9th November.

Month of November

What ends this month of October must begin this month.

On the 5th in the evening, Md. went to see the governor who was most eager that I write to my son for the arrears to be paid. He point blank refused to allow Donge to read the newspaper and the following day I wrote to ask him if this Donge might at least continue his copying.

For the rest, Md. was pleased with what he said in my regard and all this seems to be going quite well, except for the refusal of permission for the reading.

On the 5th, Montfort's bedchamber was

refurbished which caused me much loud noise.

Md. saw from the letter that Armand had written to the governor that the said Armand promised to come at the end of the year.

On the 6th, Mg. comes to make her 94th. She came in at 9 o'clock and was very good, even displayed some wit, but in spite of the submissiveness that she had sworn to me, she made it clear that there were two things that she would not do, and I realised that as a rule she would only do what she wanted in all of this. She continues to be passive and casual and even cold throughout our meeting. I can only give her one franc, she's happy with that and says sweet things about it. She had brought me a pair of stockings.

On the 8th, Rivet comes to say goodbye to us and leaves the house.

On the 10th, I saw the governor in the evening and was very pleased with our conversation. On the same day, Paquet at my request brought Isabelle back for correction. He had, he said, placed Md. de Saxe with Pigoreau, a man I greatly distrust.

On the 13th, I was expecting Mgl. Madame paid a surprise visit, stayed for quarter of an hour, and I continued to wait for Mgl.

On the 13th, the governor held a grand dinner-party to which we were not invited. On the same day, Mgl. was expected but did not come and Md. came and caused a scene, believing that she was here.

On the 14th, Mgl. sends word that she will come on Sunday the 20th.

On the 17th, I am informed that a committee is to come. That same day, Md. goes to Paris for money.

When she returns from Paris, we have some discussion with Md. but it was I who was in the wrong. Md. announces that the mother-in-law is to visit on Monday 21st.

On the 20th, Mg., who had promised to come

during mass, took time to enjoy her breakfast and instead of coming at 9 o'clock as she had promised did not come until quarter past ten. She had her period, was very lively in conversation but unfeeling in pleasures, spoke of being a governess, said that she did not wish to eat either in the kitchen or with the cook. She was not practising her handwriting which annoyed me but her reading was not bad.

I told her that truly my health had not been good for two weeks. She seemed touched by this, promised to return on Sunday the 27th and asked for some chocolate. She said that there were going to be 2 balls here, one on the feast of St. Catherine, the other on that of St. Nicholas, but she would not go to them because she knew that I would like that, and I thanked her.

On the 21st, my cousin came on her 8th visit. I was vey pleased with her. She took good note of my ailments and in a most sensitive manner, said that, if I was not prescribed some fine old wine, she would send me some herself, that the family were quite decided to bear the added costs of this treatment, but she babbled on at length, dwelling on the change of room. She went to see the governor to whom she related all the above and the very next day, Bleni came to see me and prescribed for me the treatment which I have accepted and shall follow.

My cousin speaks several times of *liberty*.

On the 22nd, I saw Bleni, he gave me a prescription. At first, the old wine was agreed and then the next day, they would only let me have 2 quarters of a bottle and all the treatment went wrong. Md. went to complain on my behalf.

Mad. makes a quick trip to Paris to fetch 78 francs.

On the same day, the 26th, Md. came back from Paris and brought back the money but no wine. She said that Boursier was waiting for his money. My pains were still very acute. The junior doctor came to arrange my suspensory bandage. That day, I had already had pain there for a week, and they hurt especially when they were touched or in the evenings.

On the 27th, Mgl. came on her 96th (visit). She seemed to be most sympathetic to my pains which I described to her in detail. She had not been to a single ball and promised not to go to any, spoke of the future, said that she would be 18 years old on the 19th of next month, lent herself as usual to our little games, promised to come back next Sunday or Monday, thanked me for what I was doing for her, and made it clear that she was not unfaithful to me, nor had she any desire to be. During this visit, Varennes brought back a reply from M. Roze who was going to put the men to work. Mgl. stayed for 2 hours, and I was very pleased with the session.

During her visit, Mg.: all the libertinism of the balls of Rousseau.

Madame confirmed to Moses that, from all that the mother-in-law had said, they could count on nothing until the Spring. Which in my opinion should take us to the 5th or 6th March, making 14 years in all and 11 years 5 or 6 days, a figure written in pencil on my door at Pelagie.

On the 30th November 1814, the leather bandage is applied for the first time.[30]

NOTES

1. On 5th June, 1807, the Minister for Police ordered all the marquis de Sade's manuscripts to be seized from rooms, including his manuscipt of *The Days At Florbelle*, which would be burned shortly after the marquis' death in 1815 by order of the Prefect of Police Delavau at the request of his son, Donatien-Claudc-Armand de Sade.
2. Sade was arrested at his publishers', Nicolas Massé's, on 6th March, 1801. The search of his rooms on 5th Jane, 1807 did in fact take place six years and 3 months later. He was transferred from Bicêtre to the asylum of Charenton-Saint-Maurice on 27th April, 1803, and the search of 5th June, 1807 was therefore carried out four years and thirty-nine days after his arrival at the asylum.
3. Georges Daumas notes that beneath the word 'fille' or 'daughter' can be made out the word 'amie' or 'female companion' crossed out. It is well known that Madame Quesnet, nicknamed "Sensible' or 'Sensitive', was allowed to live in the asylum, masquerading as the marquis's illegitimate daughter.
4. The search of June 5th, 1807 did indeed occur three years one month and five days after the search of May 1st, 1804.
5. Georges Daumas observes that the bureau in question was 'A bureau in oak with eight drawers'. It was later acquired by the board of the asylum of Charenton-Saint-Maurice.
6. Moses is a pseudonym Sade uses for himself. The 'fables' are probably either clandestine books or confidential letters. The initials M.F. are generally considered to stand for 'Ma Famille' or 'My Family'.
7. This line is very obscure. The French word 'museau', whose literal meaning is 'snout', has no metaphorical meaning other than 'mug', referring perjoratively to a person's face. Sade may be using it in the sense of 'spy'. It is also unclear who 'Le Chéri' or 'Darling' might be.
8. Varennes is a servant of the marquis's, while 'he' refers to M. de Coulmier.
9. 'f' probably stands for 'farce' or 'tall story'.

10. c.r.é: no doubt the vicar (or 'curé') of Charenton.
11. Mr Dumoustier was responsible for the internal running of the hospice.
12. The sign Ø has an erotic significance: see the introduction.
13. Mazan is a town in Provence.
14. Lenormand was a farmer on Sade's land in Versailles.
15. 'liberty' and 'Police'.
16. Sade probably means the first volume of this work.
17. Sade's cousin, Delphine, married to one of France's most powerful aristocrats, the marquis de Talaru, often exerted her considerable influence with government ministers on Sade's behalf. As a personal friend of the minister of police, Fouché, for instance, she successfully lobbied in April 1809 to prevent her cousin being transferred to one of the numbers of prisons where conditions would have been far more salubrious.
18. M.F.: see n.6.
19. Daumas points out that this note was added after the first draft.
20. Sade was actually transferred to the Bastille on the 29th February, 1784.
21. He left Charenton on the 2nd April, 1790, not the 3rd August.
22. 'ipecacuanha' is a valuable medicine produced from the root of a Brazilian plant, and it was often used as an emetic.
23. 'telegraph' or 'means of obtaining information'.
24. The illogic of this sentence is partly due to a grammatical slip on Sade's part: did he mean that he had given the copyist the manuscript for fair copying and that *the copyist* had promised to let *him* have it back?
25. Or 'new rules'?: see n.28.
26. 'poils de son con' or ' hairs of her cunt.'
27. Sade is surely miscounting here: it is Magdeleine's 90th visit.
28. It is unclear what the original French, 'au règlement', means: 'abiding by the rules' or 'up-to-date with payment' are two possibilities. The former seems more likely, if we consider the use of the same phrase at the beginning of the

entry for September 1814, which appears to allude to a ruling or a new set of rules to be made soon. This may be a reference to Sade's attempts to secure freedom, or it may concern the curtailment of Sade's movements and privileges at Charenton following the replacement of Coulmier with the less sympathetic du Maupas appointed on 31st May of that year.

29. *Le Portier des Chartreux*, a well-known pornographic classic of the eighteenth century.

30. According to the final entries in the diary, Sade had pain in his groin and testicles. The cause oft his pain, however, and therefore, the nature of the disease that killed him is far from clear.

Notes For "The Days At Florbelle"

FINAL ANALYSES AND OBSERVATIONS CONCERNING THIS GREAT WORK

[1.]
Volume One

This work begins with a title-page, a very brief editor's note, containing praise for the author and a formal admission that he is the author of *Justine*, an authorial preface addressed to libertines of every age and sex, a dedicatory epistle to God, an introduction, the name(s) of the interlocutors.

First dialogue, containing six pages. Followed then by the treatise on religion, delivered by the abbé de Modose, beginning on page 69 and ending on page 130. The second dialogue commences on p. 131 and continues till p.137, which is where the first day ends. The dissertation on the soul begins on p. 139 and continues till p. 191, where the third dialogue commences. The last day ends on the hundred and ninety-sixth page. Then comes the treatise on God which runs from p. 198 to p. 300. Then begins the fourth dialogue; it is three pages long and completes the first volume and the third day.

[2.]
Volume Two

The setting changes to a grove of myrtles and roses. We begin with a treatise on morals which goes from page 1 to page.... It is divided into eleven sections and continues till page one hundred and seventy-five. Then begins the fifth dialogue containing the adventure of the poor woodcutter. Here, the murder of the hermit is planned, and to this end he is taken to the castle dungeons, and there on page 194 ends the fifth dialogue and the fourth day. Then begins Venus Unchaste or the Art of Pleasure which starts on page 197 and runs to page... It is divided into an introduction and eleven sections.

The second volume ends midway through the ninth section, and here too ends the fifth day.

[3.]
Volume Three

It begins with the continuation of the ninth section which contains the plan for thirty-two houses of prostitution in Paris. In the tenth section is the learned treatise on antiphysics. The second part on tastes is composed of six sections, beginning on page 138 and ending on page 247.

Then the sixth dialogue begins, ending with the third volume and the sixth day. This is where the hermit is dispatched. Eudoxie is most vexed but still very fresh.

[4.]

The fourth volume contains the first fourteen chapters of the history of Modose. It ends on the seventh day. There are no dialogues.

[5.]

The fifth volume contains eleven chapters of the same history and finishes with the twenty-fifth and the eighth day. From this point, the name of Adèle is changed to Amélie. Eudoxie is seriously molested, she feels the effects on her breasts and buttocks. There are no dialogues.

[6.]

The sixth volume begins with chapter twenty-six and ends with chapter thirty-four, which completes the history of Modose and the ninth day.

In the dialogue that follows and that should start the seventh volume, Eudoxie is dispatched*.

**In the margin:* See the continuation of the analysis of the volumes on the dog-eared pages.

Plans

[7.]

After the last chapter of this story which will end the ninth day, a rare and terrible torture must begin the seventh dialogue where Eudoxie will die. After this dialogue, Modose will urge Emilie to tell her life story, which she will do in four thick volumes similar to those of the history of Modose. There will be no dialogues in the course of this narrative, but when she has finished, the eighth dialogue will commence; this will be taken from the end of the second volume of *Philosophy in the Boudoir*. Death of Mme de Mirval: to be noted according to this plan. The ninth day will finish with the history of Modose. With Amelie's first will end the tenth day which began with Eudoxie's torture without dialogue. With Amelie's second will end the eleventh day without dialogue*.

With Amelie's third will end the twelfth day without dialogue.

With Amelie's fourth and last will end the thirteenth day without dialogue. Then, the eighth dialogue will begin, but we can allow ourselves interruptions**.

* *In the margin*: This is done except for the details of the death of Mme de Mirval over which a veil has been thrown.
***In the margin*: Quite simply, the story of Adèle is complete.

[8.]

It must be noted that I intend the twenty notebooks of the story of Valrose to form the story of Amelie, and that *Amelie's woman* should narrate everything I put into *Valrose man*'s mouth***, so that the totality of this work will be composed of eight dialogues, thirteen days, a treatise on morals, one on religion, one on the soul, one on God, one on the art of jouissance, the project of thirty-two brothels for men and women for Paris, a treatise on antiphysics, and two novels, Modose's and Amelie's, in all ten large notebooks that should fill at least twenty volumes**** in print.

*** *In the margin*: Done.
**** *In the margin*:

The treatese................	3
Modose........................	3
Emile...........................	4
	10

[9.]

After a brief examination of the novel of Valrose, intended to form the memoires of Amelie de Volnange, I was very pleased with it and have written a fair copy of it. I simply noted that there were perhaps a few tedious passages in it that I might well cut, and that details of festivities should not appear at the Sénarpont house that might later be used for adventures*. Émilie must definitely be Sénarpont's niece and seduced by him**. I must confess that she works very well as a man and and I must take her through all the same situations as Valrose, sometimes as a man, sometimes as a woman. She will marry M. de Volnange in Modena, and she will have all her final adventures with him, the one in Lille, etc.***. She loses him when she returns to Europe, when she is also reunited with Roxane, with whom she comes into her ancestral inheritance at the castle of Florbelle, situated near the one which she set on fire during her childhood and in which all of this takes place.

* *In the margin*: This could not be avoided.
** *In the margin*: She can be both Sénarpont's niece and his daughter, because he will have had relations with his sister.
*** *In the margin*: None of this has been done, and things are better the way I have treated them.

Working Notes
[10.]

The Rose incident at the Jew's house must be the work of Sophie.

[11.]

Remove Zoé's name.

[12.]

Make Rose a little anxious when Modose wants to take her to the Jew's house because that is where he will destroy her.

[13.]

The woman he kills in the castle where he goes with his father is not his mother.

[14.]

Depict Sophie betraying him.*

* *In the margin*: This is done.

[15.]

When you find the passage in which Sophie saves her father's life**, insert it straight after Sophie's recapitulation on the eighteenth page of the seventh notebook.

** *In the margin*: I do not know whether this is done.

[16.]

The Jew should not tell Modose that Radzivil has killed members of his family. It is better that Radzivil tell Modose himself as he does later.

[17.]

Sophie says that she has not undergone any bad treatment at Radzivil's.

[18.]

Make it quite clear that it was Sophie who destroyed Rose at the Jew's house.

[19.]

As you read, check that you have disposed of Adrienne.

[20.]

If Sophie is treacherous, how could she have written the letters we see at the end of the second red volume?*

**In the margin*: Not yet explained.

[21.]

Bear in mind that Mme de Mirval has been sent back to Paris with Oella de Belgorod, and that she has had two children, but that you are not yet certain of the second child since she leaves pregnant with Oella**.

***In the margin*: Essential; this is mentioned again at the end.

[22.]

Do not forget to explain at the end who the old man and that young girl are that they follow everywhere.

[23.]

This interesting old man must not be called Delfrancs, since he is the father of Modose's mother and not of his father.

[24.]

Do not forget that Émilie finds Modose in Marseilles, and that she must also end her adventures in this city*.

**In the margin*: This has been done.

Notes on the History of Émilie

[25.]

I begin the fair copy on March 5th, 1806. It took me just a year to complete sixteen notebooks**.

***In the margin*: Two notebooks are finished on April 26th, nearly eight weeks; the third on May 31st, approximately one month per notebook.

8 weeks for two (a further seventy-two weeks must be needed).

18
18
18
18
72, nearly eighteen months.

This should be finished by the end of October, 1807.

The fair copy was begun on March 5th, 1806 and finished on April 25th, 1807, thirteen months and twenty days.

[26.]

I am tempted to call her Émilie de Valrose***. This must be retained on [rereading]. She is Émilie de Valrose, married name Volnange.

****In the margin*: I have done this.

[27.]

The almoner's name is Du Trochet*.

**In the margin*: Not used.

[28.]

Euphrasie: a pretty name to give her**.

***In the margin*: Used.

Essential Notes
[29.]

Cut many of Sénarpont's parties: these events work better as adventures***.

****In the margin*: Has not been done.

[30.]

The first young man is called Zirphile, the second Roselli****.

*****In the margin*: Has been to bed with her.

[31.]

There is a reference to a delicious convent in notebook IV*****.

******In the margin*: Look at it.

[32.]

Sénarpont's son is called Octave******.

****** *In the margin*: He is seriously molested; he stays

put.

[33.]

The title of Modose must be: *The Triumph of Crime, or The True History of the Abbé de Modose.*

[34.]

At the Sénarpont residence are two rooms, one of which contains twelve boys, the other twelve girls. The former have not been taken from the class of poor people, but the latter have. In one room is a scaffold and in the other a cage.

[35.]

*Women of the count***. — Catherine, wife, eighteen years; Louise, his elder daughter, seventeen; Jeanne, fifteen; and Marie, thirteen***.

** *In the margin*: Their portrait is in book IV, two pages further than the middle.
*** *In the margin*: She is no more.

[36.]

Alaïre: pretty name to find a place for****.

**** *In the margin*: It is there already.

[37.]

Do not forget Octave, left in one of the cells of the room containing the iron cage. In the other room is the scaffold.

[38.]

You have held a banquet in the room with the iron cage — hold one in the room containing the gallows.

[39.]

Characters of the orgies.

Mme de Saint-Elme, thirty-two years old; her son, fourteen; M. de Valrose, thirty-five; Milli de Valrose, fourteen; Catherine, wife, eighteen; Louise, seventeen; Jeanne, thirteen; Alaïre, daughter of Charolais, sixteen; Octave, son of the count, fifteen: eleven altogether, comprising four men and seven women.

Louis XV is twenty-eight years old, Charolais thirty-eight, Soubise thirty-five, Sénarpont thirty-three*.

**In the margin*: The cardinal, very old.

[40**.]

Since she is fifteen at Sénarpont's, say this the first evening when she says her age and when she claims to be [only] twelve or thirteen, and in general, check all the ages in this section. None of them is consistent or right, so it would be better to leave them all out.

** *In the margin*: Error.

[41***.]

Louis XV was born in 1710, so in 1739, the time when all this was taking place, he was twenty-nine or twenty-eight years old. So things are fine as they are. As for Charolais and Soubise, they could well have been ten years older.

*** *In the margin*: Essential note.

[42.]

A priest*; two choir-boys; Zirphile and Valrose dressed as devils.

Victims. — Young Saint-Elme; Octave; M. de Saint-Elme; Mme de Valrose; Alaïre, daughter of Charolais; Catherine, wife of Sénarpont; Louise and Jeanne, his daughters. Zirphile accompanies them as a Greek slave. *Agents.* — Sénarpont; Charolais; Soubise; Louis XV. There are also two old women servants and two executioners. In all, there are four torturers.

* *In the margin*: This is Cardinal Fleury.

[43.]

I have given Louis a big cock and much apathy, and Soubise more talent. The Cardinal de Fleury is present — he only fucks in the mouth**.

***In the margin*: They dine and after dinner, the executions take place.

[44.]

Note. — You must divide the work up by chapters.

[45.]

Remember that you now only have Charolais, Louis and Sénarpont with Émilie at the feast.

[46.]

It is Louis who will see himself as one of the three Graces.

[47.]

There are definitely serious errors in the chronology of ages, especially in Émilie's in relation to the ages of the King, Charolais and Sénarpont. Correct this.

[48*.]

Be careful not to repeat the adventure in the girls' convent when boarders are whipped. The journey scene must be omitted.

* *In the margin*: Essential note.

[49.]

The whole work has filled seventy-two notebooks. This means four volumes of seventeen to twenty notebooks each**.

***In the margin*:

17
17
17
<u>17</u>
68

[50.]

The first quarter of the work was completed on July

10th, 1806. It comprises seventeen notebooks and took four months and five days.

[51.]

The title is:

*The Memoires of Émile de Valrose**
or The Deviations of Libertinism

It is by laying life bare
That one brings readers back to virtue.

London, 1807.

**In the margin*: It should be *Volnange.*

[52.]

The first volume comprises seventeen notebooks and ends with the following note: Modose and Émilie spent the night together, and as the weather the next day was glorious, Mme de Valrose continued her adventures in the heart of the maze.

This first volume contains three chapters. Everything goes by chapters**.

***In the margin*: Thus ends the seventeenth notebook, the tenth day and the first volume of Valrose.

[53.]

N[ota bene]. — The chateau is called Florbelle. It would therefore be better to call her Émilie de Florbelle.

[54.]

The main title is:

Conversations at the Chateau de Florbelle,*
moral and philosophical work,
followed by
The Sacred History of the Abbot of Modose
*And of the pious memoires of Émilie de Volnange**,*
Accompanied by edifying engravings.
Holland, 1799.

* *In the margin:* Since her name after that of her husband is Volnange, it would be better to call it the chateau de Volnange.
** *In the margin:* We should put *Volnange* in the heading instead of *Valrose* to avoid having (another)[1] name ending in *ose*.

[55***.]

It should be noted that sometimes the short linking extracts from major scenes are placed at the end of volumes, sometimes at the beginning. This must be corrected so that they are always at the beginning.

*** *In the margin:* Essential.

[56****.]

Essential: — Ensure that Eudoxie is dispatched at the beginning of the story of Émilie, and put at the head of the seventh volume how the sixth ends thus.

**** *In the margin:* Very essential.

[57.]

The eighth volume, the second volume of the story of

Amélie, is read in the maze; Eudoxie is no more*.

* *In the margin:* The eighth volume is the second Volnange volume, the ninth is the third Volnange volume, and the tenth is the fourth Volnange volume.

[58.]

The fourth chapter of the story of Émile must now be commenced. — 15th July, 1806**.

** *In the margin:* Finished on the 30th.

[59.]

Correct Roxane's age. As soon as you use her at the end of the first Émilie volume as mistress of the children whipped on her shoulders, say that she is only twenty-five, seeing that you say so later***.

****In the margin*: Roxane is twenty-three years old.

[60.]

Do not say that Roxane in her story supervises Deschamps' children for five years at d'Argenson's house, as M. d'Argenson dies after a year. Say that she supervises them for a year only****.

**** *In the margin*: Error to correct in the history of Roxane.

[61*****.]

It is absolutely necessary that you make Valrose at least sixteen when Sénarpont meets her, that her adventures last twenty years, and that she be thirty-six when she finishes.

***** *In the margin*: Essential note.

[62.]

Make sure that you have not used twice the torture involving legs spread apart over a scorching fire, for you have used it with Sandieu.

[63.]

The second volume of Émilie and eighth of the whole work was completed in fair copy on the 28th October, 1806, which means that this first half took seven months less three days and thirty-four notebooks. Accordingly, it is impossible to finish the whole thing before early May, 1807*.

The second Émilie volume ends on the eleventh day, the third on the twelfth, and the third volume ends the twelfth day.

* *In the margin*: It was finished on the 25th April.

[64.]

At the convent of Turin. — Félix, twelve years old; Florentin, thirteen; Jules, fifteen; Maxime, fifteen and a half.
Hildefonse, Augustin, Anastase (uncle), Théodore, Francisque.

[65**.]

Maseline: pretty man's name to use.
Augustin must be young, as he has his mother.
The portraits of the four lords to end the forty-third

notebook.

Do not forget her entrance-exam to the class of the incendiaries of Parma, by virtue of which she undertook to make proselytes in Italy and to supervise the operations of this society.

***In the margin*: Note.

[66.]

Very essential note: — Say at the outset that her birth is mysterious and that she cannot explain it in the course of her history because of this mother and sister that I have her discover.

[67.]

Chapter X is at the beginning of the forty-eighth and [of the] fourteenth notebook.

[68.]

Valrose's name must be changed everywhere to Volnange*.

**In the margin*: But is not Volnange the name adopted?

[69.]

It is at the end of the third volume of Modose's memoires that the abbé says he knew Émilie and was involved with her. He says so very briefly in this way, concluding Émilie's memoires. You must have her arrive likewise in Marseilles, and stress this liaison a little more if you think it to the point; but if you want to have another look at the bit where Modose speaks of this, you will find it in the last sentence of the third red volume which is concluded by a romantic and tactful sentence from the priest.

[70.]

Note on Émilie's mother. — Émilie says that she has always posed as the daughter of a partisan enriched by Law's system. Her alleged father, M. de Valrose, sought his fortune as Law did and made more than ten million. But this man is not her father, and she detests him from the moment of her birth. She claims to be this M. de Valrose's only daughter, and gives him the title of marquis. Sénarpont tells her that she is both his niece and his daughter, because Mme de Valrose, Émilie's mother, is his sister and he has slept with this sister. Sénarpont's affair with this sister, who is very beautiful, was quite short-lived. Her mother is thirty-five years old when she goes to Sénarpont's and Émilie must be fifteen.

[71.]

Sénarpont had deflowered his sister at the age of seventeen, and Émilie was the result. So, Mme de Valrose can only be thirty-two* and not thirty-five as you have made her — correct this**. Émilie, née Sénarpont, was attributed to M. de Valrose. Émilie seems disposed to detest her mother, and her anger towards her excites her. She has regretted having only one mother, and would have liked to sacrifice two of them. You must not forget that trait, since you have her discover a second mother. This mother of Émilie's had saved Sénarpont's life, and that monster had prostituted her in all the bordellos of Paris. When he married her to M. de Valrose, it was in the hope of thereby becoming master and tyrant of this house. M. de Valrose knows full well that Émilie is Sénarpont's daughter. Émilie has contributed to her mother's torments: she has drunk her blood; she has caused the death of her mother by subjecting her to the Chinese torture, which consists of removing all seven layers of skin from the body; and she has devoured her heart. Therefore, it is clear that her mother did not escape and that she died at Sénarpont's chateau. These details are found at the end of the tenth notebook of Valrose's memoires.

Note at the end of this notebook all explanations relating to Émilie's birth.

**In the margin*:

$$\begin{array}{r} 17 \\ \underline{15} \\ 32 \end{array}$$

***In the margin*: Error to correct, but you must not make Émilie too young either when she finishes; the duration of her history would have been too short.

[72.]

The linking sentence is still found at the end of the volume. The second Valrose volume ends the eleventh day, and in the depths of the maze, Émilie still recounts her history right up to the end of the second volume. The third volume ends the twelfth day and the tenth chapter.

[73.]

Essential note: — Bear in mind that Émilie must always be called Volnange and never Valrose*.

**In the margin*: Another point, take care that the name is the one that has been adopted.

[74.]

The fourth volume was begun on the 21st January. It begins the thirteenth day and the eleventh chapter.

[75.]

You call her Valrose; sometimes, it's Volnange. Correct this.

[76*.]

Never call her Valrose in the course of her memoires, always Émilie. There are corrections to be made here.

**In the margin*: Essential note.

[77.]

In the fifty-ninth notebook, I think there is a contradiction. Émilie says that she can neither see nor speak secretly to Mathilde when they are both at the Jew's house, and I think that earlier, they have spoken to each other whenever they liked. Correct this if it is the case.

[78.]

I note that the stay at Noémi's is much too long.

[79.]

I notice that Mathilde behaves in Florence in a manner that is inconsistent with your portrayal of her when she arrives there.

[80.]

Fallieri's name is not spelt the same way everywhere. It

must be written as *Fallieri.*

[81.]

Take care to say that Eudoxie is the daughter of a rich merchant from Marseilles. Maintain this detail.

[82.]

In his dialogues, Modose speaks to Eugène and Flavie, one fifteen years old, the other sixteen. They are his bastard children, son [and daughter] of Mme de Mirval. He also addresses Augustin, his man-servant who is nineteen.

[83.]

Characters of the dialogues. — Émilie, thirty-two years old (should be older); Modose, her lover, thirty-eight; Eugène and Flavie, Modose's children, the former fifteen, the latter sixteen; Augustin, nineteen; Eudoxie, daughter of a rich merchant from Marseilles and friend of Émilie, seventeen; some minor characters.

[84.]

The mother of Modose's children was very beautiful. She has been sent pregnant to Paris in the care of Oella de Belgorod.

[85.]

After sixty-six pages of dialogue, Modose reads the piece entitled 'Religion'. This piece, 'Religion', extends from 69 to 130.

Then, the dialogues continue again until 134. This ends the first day.

The beginning of the second is the piece on the soul which goes from 139 to 192*.

The dialogues continue again from 192 to 197. Then Modose continues the piece on God which goes from 198 to 300.

Five pages of dialogues complete the first volume.

**In the margin*: All this is in an earlier note.

[86.]
Second volume

The treatise on morals starts the second volume and extends to page 174. It is divided into sections. Then begins the fifth dialogue, in which Eudoxie shows herself to be still a little prudish. This dialogue contains the encounter with a woodcutter, and it ends with the detention of the holy hermit. Then begins the Art of Pleasure which extends from page 199 until the end of the second volume, which ends the fifth day.

[87.]
Third volume

Venus Unchaste or the Art of Pleasure continues at the start of the third volume up to page 247. This dissertation ends with the cries of the hermit. These are redoubled.... loudly. Then comes the sixth dialogue which lasts eighteen or twenty pages and ends the third volume. In this dialogue, Eudoxie is strongly threatened by Modose, Modose's children prove themselves to be profoundly libertine, and Eudoxie is whipped. It is here that the hermit is put to the question. He is made to undergo a thousand horrors (in this scene, Flavie shows herself to be very cruel), and his torture lasts seven hours. Eudoxie is still alive. She has been abused, but she is still quite healthy and still clings to her antiquated notions. This volume ends with Adèle's promise to recount her adventures, and her story begins the fourth volume. This is the girl whose first seven notebooks have been burnt and the end removed. It is rewritten in seventy-two notebooks and forms four thick volumes.

[88.]
Seventh volume

At the beginning of the seventh volume in the dialogue that ends the sixth and starts the seventh can be found the death of Eudoxie and the first three chapters of the history of Amélie de Valrose.

[89.]
Eighth volume

The eighth volume contains the fourth chapter of the history of Amélie.

[90.]

I think that two tortures have been forgotten:
The rack by means of which all limbs can be compressed at will, even the victim's whole body, at will and by degrees. Someone works the rack and four libertines jerk themselves off as they watch.

The other one is the porphyry vase into which the victim wants to shit. This vase is in a large gallery where the victim is expected. As soon as she has done the business, she is driven forward with heavy blows from a police whip, a trap-door gives way, and she falls onto burning coals where she is consumed.

[91.]

Here is the speech by Hélène de Sénarpont to Émilie:

— I recognise you as my daughter from your name and from the mark that you bear on your left arm. These are the facts. Sénarpont had two sisters: Hélène de Sénarpont and Thérèse de Sénarpont.

I am the first, Thérèse the second, and it was Thérèse that Sénarpont married off to M. de Valrose. Sénarpont slept with both his sisters and had a daughter by each one. One was named Émilie — that's you; the other Félicité — that's the girl who is with me, but Félicité is Thérèse's daughter and you are mine. I shall clarify further the reasons for this deception. Sénarpont wanted to do with his two daughters what he had done with his two sisters, but his intention was to sacrifice the least pretty of the two children very early to his destructive passion, and to allow the other one to reach the age of beauty. You were the one most favoured by nature, the one who showed most promise. Consequently, he had Félicité secretly snatched from her cradle and put you in her place, so that, being raised by his sister, Thérèse de Valrose, you might in some way be protected from his passions, at least, as I told you just now, until the age of fifteen or sixteen, which he felt himself to be incapable of doing if you had stayed with me whom he kept with him. As soon as Félicité was seven years old (and though without daring to say as much, I had realised that she was not my daughter, since she did not bear the mark on her arm that proved she was mine), as soon, I say, as she had reached the age of seven, Sénarpont revealed to me his unspeakable intentions, and this is what saved us both. You know the rest of our adventures. I simply wanted to prove, as I have just done, that you are my daughter and not Thérèse's, and that you are Félicité's sister, since she is, like you, the daughter of the marquis de Sénarpont, which, by virtue of this terrible man's crimes, makes you both sisters and first cousins.

In the margin: Hélène, Thérèse, Félicité, Émilie.

[92.]
Reminders

On finishing the narration of Roxane's story to Zolbar, you must explain the reasons why the captain of the ship maintained that she was worth more than a hundred thousand écus to him.

You must also break off all her contacts with this period, so that the editor's note is found to be accurate, and that she does not nor cannot locate anyone, in order that any desire to continue this story be removed.

[93.]

The flame under the cunt is used two or three times: it must be cut out, and left only at the chateau de Colli.

[94.]

You must also cut out the desecrations of the host at Sénarpont's house, keeping it in only for when he has adventures.

[95.]

There would be no harm either in cutting out everything relating to the convent and its boarders in Sénarpont's parties; all of this can be moved to his adventures later.

Generally speaking, Sénarpont's parties are too splendid for the beginning.

[96.]

Do not start Valrose off so young, or else spin out the time more, for in the eighth book he is barely twenty years old, if you make him come to Florbelle at the age of thirty-six. Spin out the time more in Modena. When Roxane begins telling her story to Zolbar, make sure she says that it was Joseph who had betrayed them, have her say that she persuaded Sandieu of this, for otherwise, this betrayal would be blamed on Valrose. I believe you have him stay in Modena for three years — you could have him remain there longer; he arrived there at the age of twenty-five.

[97.]

Follow exactly all the reminders on the grey pages.

[98.]

I think I stopped at the story of the woman in the chateau de Charmeille. It is this story that, with some cutting and adjusting, will form Roxane's story*.

**In the margin*: The whole of this forms the history of Madame de Valrose.

[99.]

Remember to emphasise more [the] dead body that was buried at the Dominicans, on the day when Valrose held a party in the cellars, for in the story of Adrienne, the murder of this monk is mentioned. Point out at this party that this monk had just been killed. It is the same that caused a catastrophe in Turin in Adrienne's adventures, but remember that it was not the Dominicans — change this.

You should have put in a discourse on the idea that one must never resist the inclinations that one has received from nature, the reason for the contradictions that are perceivable between the heart and the head.

Do not forget that cardinal de Fleury lost the navy in France. It was he who replaced the duke at the ministry, who as father of the present Condés, must have been Charolais's brother. He must dislike the cardinal, and Sénarpont must act as go-between between the two. The cardinal died at his country residence at Issy.

[100.]

Valrose is twenty-eight* when he arrives in Florence, and Mathilde twenty-two.

**In the margin*: I have made him thirty years old.

[101.]

You have made Roxane too old at the beginning. She absolutely must be Valrose's age.
Mathilde must be six years younger than him, and Roxane deals tactfully with him (essential).

Roxane, arrested with Sandieu, escapes and passes him off as her husband. They separate. She becomes [mistress?] of a [of the?] cardinal; it is at this point that she takes up her story again.

[102.]
Diverse characters

Men. — Octave; Théodore; Anastase; Félix; Léon; Jules; Maxime; Brisetout (Breakall); Coeurderiche (Richheart); Valrose; M. de Valrose; Dorvil[le], Valrose's friend; the marquis de Sénarpont; the cardinal de Fleury; the comte de Charolais, going by the name of Jaco; Dupont, almoner; Soubise, Louis XV; Sandieu; Joseph; Sicardi, François, Gonsalvi, Clément his son, smugglers; Father Ambroise, capuchin monk; Ligni, lover of Adrienne; Noémi, Jew; Falconi, secretary to the duke of Tuscany; Frédéric, second duke of Tuscany; Fillieri; Forli; Crève-coeur (Heartbreaker); Lisle de Zorlan; Auguste; Guillaume; Jacques; Robert.[2]

Women. — Madame de Valrose; Adrienne de Valrose; Madame de Dorville; Gertrude; Adélaïde; Suzanne; Laurentia; Virginie; Rosa; Catherine, wife of Sénarpont; Louis, Jeanne, Marie, daughters of Sénarpont; Zoloé; Angélique; the marquise de Roseville; Claire, Sophie, her daughters; Clotilde, chambermaid; Eudoxie; Neuville; Clémentine; Aglaé; Cécile; Rosine; Adélaïde [de] Forlis; Victorine du Ponceau; Mother Sainte-Thérèse; Émilie [?] du Faille; Madame de Nauzel; Angélique [de] Dorville; Olympe, Marguerite, [chamber?]maid and daughter of Madame de Mauzel; Charlotte; Blaisine; Ursule; Iseleau; Adélaïde et Gertrude de Nanteuil; Roxane; Isabelle Gonsalvi; Madame Léonard; Donna Héléna; Mathilde; Fortunée de Modène; Eugénie; Ruth, Moabie, Judith, Rebecca, sisters of Noémi; Mother Aldegonde; Mother Félicité; Mother Sainte-Thècle; Mother Sainte-Aure; Suzanne; Laurentie, wife of Forli; Virginie; Roza; Brigide; Zingua, queen of Angola; Zolba, her confidante; Zoé; Eloïe; Isménie; Énoi; Zoldorie; Bolema; Zordis; Ambroisine, daughter of Valrose.

[103.]

Valrose has killed: his father, his mother, his mistress, his mistress's father, his mistress's sister, his wife, his father-in-law, his daughter, and many victims. But he has always been faithful to friendship and has never done anything against his two friends, Roxane and Mathilde, nor against François.

[104.]
Parties thrown for Sénarpont

The Callipyge temple of Venus.

The thieves' cave where mass is said.

Bethlehem where he finds Jesus, his mother and Élisabeth.

The mystery of the good goddess.

Thieves, murders and highway holdups.

Theft and murder committed against one person by Jaco.

Burbate or sodomite temple of Venus.

Convent of young boarders where there is whipping.

Meeting with the executioner's cart taking women to the guillotine. They publicly execute seven, including one who is pregnant.

They whip little boys in a boarding-house.

Farm where they fuck animals. They cut the throats of new-born children in their mothers' arms.

Farm where stallions, horses and bulls fuck women.

Four pregnant and naked whores being birched.

The men amuse themselves with the soldiers who execute them.

Anosia temple of Venus, or Venus cruel; here, nine sacrifices occur in three days. It is here that Roxane recounts her adventures.

They meet up with a slave-trader. They hurl four of them onto the rocks.

Temple of Bacchus where human sacrifices are carried out, a bull-fight featuring women, and different firework displays where children are carried off [sic] by bombs and rockets.

Delicious force.

Joséphine or the unhappy wife, a comedy.

Park full of children upon whom they throw themselves. Women used as targets: arrows are fired at them. Woman hunt.

[105.]

In order to enjoy what I shall give you, mademoiselle, the holy man said to me, perhaps I ought to believe you to be profoundly convinced by the great truths of our holy religion, but unfortunately, I already know all about your frightful principles, and I must fear failure in my undertaking. Yet, I shall dare to tell you, mademoiselle, that one has to be awfully blind to reject the great and sublime truths of the Christian religion. How can one not see that it can only be the work of God? and if one accepts this holy and sublime God, how can one not think him to be extraordinarily angered by the crimes that men indulge themselves in on earth? If God is the model of virtue, how could he not detest vice? If he detests it, how could he not punish it? What do we admire in the works of the Almighty? Is it not the profound order which preserves and governs all that he has created? and is it not in this sublime order that we recognise the image of a God? Now, if he loves order, if he makes order the reigning principle, whoever disturbs this order..

....

NOTES

[1] My parenthesis.
[2] My parentheses.

Charenton Letters

To Charles Quesnet

Consider, my friend, that your mother's existence divided itself to bring your own into being: this existence which you enjoy is strictly speaking just an emanation of hers. How much, for me, such a reflection, though drawn from the physical alone, should increase the moral sentiments you owe this creature, sacred to you in so many ways! Consider, my friend, that the debt of respect and affection that you owe her is nothing in comparison with the care she has taken of you, and that, in a word, it is never in our power to pay back, to recompense a mother for all that she has done for us since she gave us life in her loins. Often have I told you, a mother is a friend that nature gives us only once, and for whom nothing in the world can compensate when we have had the misfortune to lose her. We find nothing else that can take her place: the poisonous traits of men, their wickedness, their calumnies wound us unimpeded. We hurl ourselves into the bosom of a friend, of a spouse; but how different, my dear Quesnet! We do not meet there with the disinterested attentions of a mother, that precious sensibility untainted by any self-interest; in a word, oh my dear friend, those are not the hands of nature.

To Gaufridy

Summer, 1803

Before beginning my letter, monsieur, I feel the need to justify myself in your eyes with regard to several faults that you seem to ascribe to me, although I can assure you that, for my part, I do not believe you to be guilty of any, and that events and circumstances are the sole causes of these faults which I merely appear to possess.

I have never withdrawn my trust in you, my dear lawyer, allow me this old expression of our very long relationship, but the sale of La Coste alienated you greatly from the little I have remaining in the 'Comtat' as it used to be known. This circumstance, combined with your antipathy for travelling, naturally and in spite of myself, as it were, took the management of this part of my property out of your hands. The administration of this fell henceforth to a man from Carpentras. Courtois could manage Mazan on his own. As for Arles, you did not wish to... or rather, you could not. Whom did you offer me to replace you? Your elder son whose letters alone put my temperature up for a week. I therefore had to take the decision that I took. Reason, propriety, everything dictated this to me. My heart alone opposed it, but there are so many occasions in life when the promptings of the heart must be resisted. Perfectly certain that you were not attached to the miserable and very meagre interest of your administration, I had calculated that, whether it was yours or not, we could love each other all the same, and your obstinate silence since that time has proven to me how wrong I was. I consoled myself by thinking often of you, and by speaking of you many times during the year with the sincere lady friend to whom you have just written and who has always seen it as her duty to remain a constant friend to you. As proof of the desire I had to receive news of you, I have repeatedly asked after you in my letters to Courtois who, in truth, has never given me the satisfaction of a reply. For your part, during this long interval I have had proof of your remembrance and your attachment, and I remind you of it here, both to thank you for it and to ask you to carry it into effect. Sambuc de la Coste wrote to me five years ago to tell me that you had charged him to let me know that you had in your possession a few of my papers which had escaped the looting and were in your safe-keeping, and which you wished to return to me if I provided you with a safe opportunity to do so. I thank you with all my heart for this service and beg you to fulfil this promise, wishing very much to have these papers again, and here are the means that I can offer you by which you may pass them on to me. You must send them, either by hand or by coach or through the post if they are not too bulky, to M. Lenormand, wood-merchant, boulevard de l'Impératrice, n° 101, in Versailles, département de Seine-et-Oise, with the sole proviso that you warn this gentleman by letter a week in advance that he is to receive a package for me containing farm leases and other property papers necessary to my business affairs. Please ask him to pass them on to me immediately, having first acknowledged receipt. Do not worry about the cost, I am too desirous to retrieve these items to bother about one écu more or less, although this vehement wish on my part should not prevent you from adopting the most economical method provided that it is the safest. Above all, please include in this parcel a very inaccurate and crude manuscript of my life memoirs which I have seen in your younger son's hands and which he has always refused to give back to me. I completely disown this manuscript and I beg you to have it returned to me. I am now going to answer a reflection which doubtless occurs to you concerning the time I have taken to ask you for these papers mentioned by Sambuc and which I am requesting from you so earnestly today. I was waiting.... I was myself carried away by circumstances which did not allow me any such diversion. The moment has arrived, and I was about to write to you when your very kind letter to Madame Quesnet arrived. Let us then talk of this, a little late since it is strictly speaking the principal motive of this letter. Madame Quesnet writes on this same occasion to thank you for the great discretion which you have just shown her. Please likewise accept my own heartfelt gratitude for this, and I most earnestly beg you to handle this affair with all the intelligence and industry that you can muster, in order at least to maintain on behalf of this honest and precious friend the just rights that she possesses to my property. I shall, then, expect this favour from you without further ado, since it is to your heart that I have just appealed, and since, when your memories are directed by your sentiments, you can forget nothing. I have, besides, one further request to make of you regarding this matter.

You have undoubtedly seen the excessive claims of madame de Sade with some surprise. I recall an extremely interesting note from you regarding these ridiculous claims which belittled them in an unanswerable fashion. Unfortunately, I have mislaid this document, and at this moment, I find myself in circumstances in which I have urgent need of it. Would it be possible for you to send it to me again? I should be most obliged if you could! Try, do, to render me this service, I beg you. I am on the point of completing a transaction with my children by virtue of which I give away everything for an income of... and, as they inordinately inflate their mother's claims, I am in the greatest need of this paper which can provide me with the means to diminish them. This sale of Madame Rovère's is going to lead to a very great court action between the stubborn Madame de Sade and this respectable lady, action in which there is talk no less of expropriating from me acquisitions I made with *the Rovère money*. Can one do this? Please advise me on this. And now please be good enough to answer a few questions, the first of which interest me enormously and the others doubtless less, though sufficiently, however, for me to be grateful to you for answering them.

How goes everything with you? Has life been kind to you and your family, have you been able to set your sons up well, have you found good marriages for your daughters?

How is the good and honest Madame Gaufridy? And you, my dear lawyer, you, my contemporary in life, my childhood companion, how are you?

There we are, that's the most interesting part. Now for the rest.

A few details about la Coste, about those I have loved, about the Paulets, etc.

Is it true that Madame Rovère is keeping the château for herself? What state is the château in? And my poor gardens, is there still anything left of me in them?

How are my relations in Apt?

Now, perhaps, you would like to hear a word about me? Well, *I am not happy*, but I am in good health. This is all I can say in answer to a friend who, I hope, may still inquire after me.

Ever yours, SADE.

Do not attribute our delay in replying to idleness. This delay is due solely to the length of time your letter took to reach us, given our numerous changes of residence over the last five years and our retirement to the country for the last three.

Our address is: House of M. de Coulmiers, president of the canton and member of the Legion of Honour, at Charenton-Saint-Maurice, department of the Seine.

To Monseigneur Fouché,
Minister for the National Police Force,
Sade, Man of Letters

12th August, 1804 (24 Thermidor, year XII)

Monseigneur,

I have been improperly deprived of my freedom for nearly four years, and it is only thanks to a particular philosophy that I have been able to bear until this day the various vexations I am forced to undergo on pretexts that are as frivolous as they are absurd.

The laws and regulations with regard to individual liberty have never been so openly infringed as in my own case, since it is without trial or any legal process whatever that the authorities persist in keeping me locked up, allegedly because of an obscene work that is wrongly attributed to me, and also because of a number of tales that people like to imagine and ascribe to my private life, *and all of this without foundation*.

Consequently, monseigneur, I find myself obliged to have recourse to your authority and above all to your fairness, *to obtain my release*, since not only are all laws and reason ignored as far as I am concerned, but also because, according to the letter of both, I should be set free.

I dare to hope, monseigneur, that you will deign to take account of the just demands of a sexagenarian to whom all that is dearest it is in your power to grant.

I have the honour respectfully to be your Excellency's most humble and most obedient servant,

SADE

Last Proposals...
24th August, 1805

Last proposals made to my family upon acceptance of which I promise to sign immediately the transaction the plan of which has been sent to me. It will be clear from a reading of this how little I deviate from this plan, enclosed herewith.

For the assignment of all my property I am awarded an income of five thousand francs which I accept.

Mme Quesnet is awarded twenty thousand francs instead of the thirty-five thousand that are due to her - she accepts this, but I would ask that this sum bear interest at five per cent from the day when the deed is signed. In this alone do I encounter *an obstacle, and one that should not be created by children who know the sacred origin of this debt.*

I have asked for fifteen thousand francs for my unsecured creditors, my debts amounting to this sum. I am offered only nine, which I accept, but on condition that the family reach a settlement with them and that the ill temper that will result from the reduction of what is owed to them should not rebound upon me.

Monsieur de Coulmiers and the few debts I have here will be paid at once from present income, so that I shall be entirely acquitted of what is due at Charenton upon signing.

My income of 5000 francs and that of 1000 francs awarded to Mme Quesnet shall be paid to us as suggested in four advance payments every three months.

These two annuities shall not be distrainable, and shall always be paid in cash wherever I live. They shall be exempt from any kind of tax or deduction whether present or future.

I shall retain the château of Saumane and its

outbuildings, with the undertaking never to sell it, but it is my wish that Mme Quesnet may end her days there if she so desires.

I shall retain any ground rents paid.

I reserve the right upon my death to make over 800 francs income to whoever cares for me during my final hours, this to be payable only for the lifetime of this person.

The income of twenty thousand francs to Mme Quesnet shall revert to her son for the child's lifetime only.

Mme Quesnet shall not be able to assign either her income or her annuity, both of these items being made unassignable by the deed, and she shall be required by this same deed to spend this income with me during my lifetime, in default of which said income would cease to be revertible to her son.

Both incomes must be distrainable from the farmers before one has the right to take a single sol from said farmers, and it must be stated in the deed that I am considered to have cleared my debts to madame de Sade and her children, and *these clauses in addition to the deed itself must be signed by the mother and the three children.*

The payments will be prescribed at a reputed and honest notary's, and *I reserve the right to repossess my properties upon the least failure to observe either of the clauses of said transaction.*

The notary charged with my income shall pay it to my order by money-draft, regardless of my circumstances, situation or domicile.

If desired, one of the Beauce lands could be assigned to Mme Quesnet, again with the precaution that it be made unassignable. In that case, she would be responsible for her twenty thousand francs and for nine thousand francs to the unsecured creditors. Now, this land which is scarcely worth twenty to twenty-five thousand francs, would therefore discharge twenty-nine. Mme Quesnet would therefore pay the creditors with the income from the land, and the annuity would still be ours as well as the income when the debts were paid. Under these conditions, Mme Quesnet's twenty thousand francs would no longer be required to bear interest.

This ultimatum must be acknowledged to be much more moderate than last year's, since only one difficulty remains, that of having interest paid on Mme Quesnet's twenty thousand francs. As can be seen, I bow to reason with regard to all the rest but I absolutely cannot bend on this clause.

Sade
The 6th Fructidor Year XIII

To Gaufridy

December, 1807

I still augur sufficiently well, monsieur, in spite of my failings, of the kindness and attention with which you have handled the affairs of madame Quesnet and myself in the past, to hope that you might render the said lady the service explained herewith, and for which she and I shall be eternally grateful to you. This is the matter in question.

According to the new law governing mortgage registrations dated September last, the word *due* must appear at the head of the registration schedule.

Consequently, madame Quesnet begs you to check whether this word appears in her schedules and if it does not appear, please to get it put in, and in addition to this kind service on your part, to send an abstract of it.

Should there be any expenses to pay, please be good enough to pay them in advance, send the bill with your reply, and I shall immediately send you a draft payable by M. Courtois who will honour it on demand.

Since your son has been in Paris, I have had the pleasure of seeing him on three occasions only. But I know that he is in good company, that he is using the time profitably and in ways such that you can only congratulate yourself on having made sacrifices for his trip.

Please do remember madame Quesnet and myself to all of your dear, kind family, let us have news of them and of your good self, and accept my most sincere best wishes for a prosperous and happy New Year.

I am forever your sincere and faithful servant and friend.

SADE. This 23rd December, 1807

To Napoléon Bonaparte

To His Majesty The Emperor and King, Protector of the Confederation of the Rhine, Presiding on the Committee for Petitions to the Council of State

17th June 1809

Sire,

M. de Sade, father to several children among whom he has the consolation of being able to count a son who is serving with distinction in the armed services, has been leading the most unhappy of existences for more than nine years in three different prisons in succession. He is a septuagenarian, nearly blind, afflicted with gout and rheumatism in his chest and stomach which cause him to suffer horrible pains. Certificates from physicians at the house of Charenton where he is presently attest to the truth of these facts and authorise him to request that he be set free at long last, vowing that there shall never be cause to repent having done so.

He dares to consider himself, Sire, with the very deepest respect, Your Majesty's most humble and most obedient servant and subject.

DE SADE

To Madame Cochelet, companion of the Queen of Holland

Performance of the 23rd May 1810

Madame,

The interest that you have appeared to take in the dramatic recreations of the inmates of my house makes it imperative for me to offer you tickets for each and every one of their performances.

Spectators such as yourself, Madame, have such a powerful effect on their self-esteem that in the very hope of captivating and pleasing you, they find every means of exalting their imagination and nurturing their talents.

On Monday next, the 28th of this month, they are performing *The Spirit of Contradiction, Marton and Frontin* and *The Two Gentlemen of Savoy*.

I await your orders for the dispatch of any tickets that you may require, and cordially ask you to pay my respects to the ladies of the court of Her Majesty the Queen of Holland, a princess whose rare and precious qualities are so delightfully able to capture the hearts of all Frenchmen and so to win devotion as sincere from them as from those over whom she reigns.

SADE

To Monsieur de Coulmier

1810

I have the honour to greet monsieur de Coulmier and to send him the list that we have agreed between us. He is urgently requested to approve it, since no one wishes to incur any costs and above all run up any bill without having secured the approval of his boss for his plans.

Here is, monsieur, a formal request from M. and Mme de Roméi whom I have had the honour to mention to you, and who are entered on the list that I have presented to you.

I should be very much obliged to you if you would not refuse them.

Respectfully your devoted servant.

SADE

List amended by the governor:

M. Treillard..3 seats
Mme Ronchoux, rue de Choiseul, no 13...............2 seats
Mme Cochelet, companion of the Queen of Holland........
....8 seats
Mme d'Houdetot.. 3 seats
The Irish doctor..1 seat
The Sauvan household.. 4 seats
The Finot household..2 seats
The de Guise household.. 3 seats
Mme Lambert... 3 seats
Mme Gonax..4 seats
The priest, for M. Norvert.....................................4 seats
The mayor of Charenton....................................... 2 seats
The mayor of Les Carrières...................................1 seat
M. Millet... 1 seat

Mme Quesnet	7 seats
M. de Sade	7 seats
M. du Camp	3 seats
Mlle Adélaide	3 seats
Mme de Huteuil	5 seats
M. Le Roi	2 seats
Mme Urbistondos	6 seats
M. Vivet	2 seats
M. Chapron	3 seats
M. Veillet	4 seats
Mme Marchand	2 seats
M. Le Couteux	2 seats
M. Florimond	2 seats
Three de Nogent ladies	3 seats
M. Flandrin	1 seat
	90 seats
Charenton employees	36 seats
Patients	60 seats
	186 seats

To Monsieur de Coulmier

(December 1810)

I ask M. de Coulmier:

1. To let me be master of the key to my chamber, save for the first door in the corridor which alone shall be locked from 10 o'clock in the evening until 7 o'clock in the morning;

2. To allow me to take walks *without being followed* at those hours in the day that suit me best, as long as the garden is open;

3. To let me converse freely with the three persons mentioned below, and to do so exclusively, that is, *I undertake to speak to no other person*: Mme Blotfière, my neighbour, M. de Savines, my relative, and M. de Léon;

4. Finally, to have all the pens and paper that have recently been taken from me returned to me.

SADE

To Monsieur de Coulmier

3rd March 1813

I would ask you, monsieur, with the utmost urgency, to give Mme Quesnet the chamber above me, *which you have led my son to expect would be done*. My tranquillity and my health depend upon it. If only you knew how much I suffer when this chamber is occupied by people who, believing themselves (with reason) to be masters of their own living space, do not for that reason alone imagine that they owe me any consideration... Yes, monsieur, I do assure you that if you knew what suffering this causes me, I feel sure that in view of the friendship you have always shown me, you would certainly not do this.

I beg you to take account finally of my request, and to accept my most sincere gratitude.

Your most humble and most obedient servant.

SADE

Do not forget to send for the fifteen hundred *livres* that M. Boursier the notary, of the rue Grenier-Saint-Lazare, has for you.

To the Directors of the Théâtre-Français

(End of 1813)

I have the honour to present to the directors of the Théâtre-Français a tragedy in five acts, the subject of which seems to me to suit the present circumstances. This play was read in this theatre on the 14th November 1791 and accepted with amendments. These were done, and it is this amended version which I am offering to you for the second time. Mlle Raucourt, Monsieur Saint-Prix and Monsieur Saint-Fal must remember this work, extracts of which I had read to them in private before reading it to the committee. Apart from several minor plays of secondary interest, I still have three strong pieces in my portfolio, five-act plays in verse, one of which was unanimously accepted and ensured my access to the stage for three years.

I am asking here for neither protection nor indulgence, but am relying on your fairness. You will accept me if you find me worthy, and the sentiments which your talents inspire in me will be neither increased nor diminished by rejection or acceptance.

I remain always, messieurs, your most humble and most obedient servant.

To Monsieur Coulmier

(Beginning of 1814)

I have the honour to greet Monsieur de Coulmier, and I entreat him to leave me the man he has given me, and not to make me suffer the nuisance, which I find appalling, of seeing a different face every day.

SADE

To Monsieur Roulhac du Maupas

5th November 1814

His honour the Governor does not wish Mr Donge, head of the lottery office, to come and relieve Mme Quesnet's eyes and my own by reading the newspaper to us - nothing simpler. I am far from wishing to infringe any rule. But this good man from the lottery has undertaken to make a few copies of dramatic works for me. These have been accepted by different theatres and all approved by the police. I urgently request that he be allowed to continue, for both he and I would lose much from this interruption. At the same time, may I point out that if he were to continue this work, Mr Donge would be obliged to work for only one hour, once a week only, for two months only.

I present my respects to His Honour the Governor, and again urgently request that he not inconvenience me by refusing me this trifle. I am going to write to my son in accordance with His Honour's wishes.

To Monsieur Pépin

November 1814

Monsieur Pépin,
Proprietor at Saumane,
par L'Isle,
at L'Isle, department of Vaucluse

My dear Monsieur Pépin,

More than six weeks ago, I sent an authorisation to M. Roze, all legal and correct, requiring my wood to be cut and the funds sent to me immediately, given that it was only my desperate need of money that urged me to press for this to be done. However, I have heard nothing, and you yourself, with whom I asked M. Roze to negotiate, have not contacted me regarding this matter.

I should therefore be obliged if, once you have received my letter, you would see M. Roze to discover from him what the reasons for his silence can be. Please inform me straightaway what the situation is and dispatch the work quickly if it has not yet been undertaken. M. Roze was also directed in the same letter to have Broselli pay out of this money any postal charges that I may owe yourself and M. Roze, as well as any other petty expenses; also, with the same money, to make any repairs urgently needed at the château, and to send me the balance by bill of exchange drawable in Paris. However, none of any of this is being done, and I confess to you that I am amazed. I beg you to clear all this up for me and to advise me of the situation by return post. If nothing has been undertaken, hurry things along, for the need I have of this money is beyond words, and above all, ensure that M. Roze gets the best possible price for this wood.

Broselli will remain until any new instructions, since the man I wished to send you did not want to set off for parts totally foreign to him.

I embrace you and all that is dear to you with all my heart, and beseech you to send me news of M. Roze and his transactions as soon as possible.

DE SADE

At Charenton, this 11th November 1814

M. Roze should please pay M. Pépin the postal charges of this letter, which has not been franked, from the money which he is to realise for me.

DE SADE

The Last Will And Testament

LAST WILL AND TESTAMENT
of Donatien Alphonse François Sade
Man of Letters

I rely upon the filial piety of my children for the execution of the clauses set out below, wishing that their own children may act with regard to them as they will have done with regard to me.

First: Wishing to bear testimony to Mademoiselle Marie-Constance Renelle (Sade writes Reinelle), wife of Monsieur Balthasar Quesnet, believed deceased, wishing, I say, to bear testimony to this lady, insofar as my meagre means allow, of my extreme gratitude for the devotion and sincere friendship that she has shown me since the twenty-fifth of August seventeen hundred and ninety until the day of my death, feelings shown by her not only with tact and unselfishness, but what is more, with the most courageous energy, since under the regime of the Terror she rescued me from the revolutionary blade suspended all too surely above my head, as everyone knows; for the reasons explained above, I therefore give and bequeath to the said lady Marie-Constance Renelle, wife of Quesnet, the sum of twenty-four thousand *livres* in cash from the Tours mint, being legal tender in France at the time of my demise, with the wish and intention that this sum be deducted from the freest and the most unattached part of my legacy, charging my children to deposit it within the space of one month from the day of my demise with Monsieur Finot, notary at Charenton-Saint-Maurice, whom I name for this purpose executor of my will and whom I charge to use the said sum in the most secure manner that is at the same time the most advantageous to madame Quesnet and likely to provide her with an income sufficient to feed and keep her, which income shall be paid to her punctually each and every quarter, shall be untransferable and unattachable by any person whatever. Desiring, moreover, that the principal and the income from the above-mentioned sum be revertible to Charles Quesnet, son of the said dame Quesnet, who shall become owner of the entire bequest under the same conditions but only following the demise of his worthy mother.

And this desire which I express here with regard to the legacy made by me to Madame Quesnet, in the unlikely event that my children should seek to evade or shirk their responsibility, I beg them to remember that they had promised the said dame Quesnet a roughly similar sum in recognition of the care she has taken of their father, and as this deed merely concurs with and anticipates their original intentions, my mind is not perturbed even for an instant by doubts that they will comply with my final wishes, especially when I think of those filial virtues that they have never failed to display and that render them worthy of all my paternal affections.

Second: In addition, I give and bequeath to the said dame Quesnet all the furniture, effects, linen, clothing, books or papers that shall be found in my rooms on the occasion of my death, with the exception, however, of my father's papers which shall be identified as such by labels attached to the bundles and which shall be handed over to my children.

Third: It is also my intention and my last wish that this bequest should in no way deprive Madame Marie-Constance Renelle, wife of Quesnet, of any rights, claims or dues that she may wish to make upon my estate, whatever the grounds may be.

Fourth: I give and bequeath to Monsieur Finot, the executor of my will, a ring to the value of twelve hundred *livres* in return for the trouble he will have taken in executing this deed.

Fifth: Lastly, I absolutely forbid anyone to cut my body open on any pretext whatsoever. I ask most earnestly that it be kept in the chamber where I shall have died for forty-eight hours, then placed in a wooden coffin which shall not be nailed shut until the above-mentioned period of forty-eight hours has elapsed, whereupon the said coffin shall be nailed shut. During this interval, an express message shall be sent to Monsieur Le Normand, wood-merchant, of number one hundred and one, boulevard de l'Égalité, Versailles, asking him to come himself with a cart to fetch my body, and to transport it under his own escort in the said cart to the wood on my lands at Malmaison near Épernon in the commune of Émancé, where I wish it to be laid, without ceremony of any kind, in the first copse on the right as one enters this wood from the old château by the broad path dividing it. A ditch shall be dug in this copse by the tenant-farmer of Malmaison under the supervision of Monsieur Le Normand who shall not leave my body until after he has placed it in the said ditch. He may, if he wishes, be joined in this ceremony by those among my relatives or friends who, without pomp of any kind, shall have been good enough to show me this last mark of affection. Once the ditch has been covered over, it shall be strewn with acorns so that in time, as the earth upon the said ditch becomes green again and the copse grows back as dense as it was before, the traces of my grave may disappear from the face of the earth as I trust my memory shall fade from the minds of men, except, however, for that small number who have been kind enough to love me until the last and of whom I carry a sweet remembrance with me to the grave.

Done at Charenton-Saint-Maurice in sound mind and body this thirtieth day of January eighteen hundred and six.

D. A. F. Sade

Also available from Creation Books:

PHILOSOPHY IN THE BOUDOIR

The Marquis de Sade

In the boudoir of a sequestered country house, a young virgin is ruthlessly schooled in evil. Indoctrinated by her amoral tutors in the ways of sexual perversion, fornication, murder, incest, atheism and complete self-gratification, she takes part with growing abandon in a series of violent erotic orgies which culminates with the flagellation and torture of her own mother – her final act of liberation. *Philosophy In The Boudoir* is the most concise, representative text out of all the Marquis de Sade's works, containing his notorious doctrine of libertinage expounded in full, coupled with liberal doses of savage, unbridled eroticism, cruelty and violent sexuality. The renegade philosophies put forward here would later rank amongst the main cornerstones of André Breton's Surrealist manifesto. This new edition includes *The Lusts Of The Libertines*, a brand new, unexpurgated and explicit translation of the 447 "complex, criminal and murderous lusts" of the Libertines as documented by de Sade in his accursed atrocity bible *The 120 Days Of Sodom*; a catalogue of debaucheries, cruelties and pathological perversions still unequalled in the annals of transgressive literature.

www.creationbooks.com